To P. 18 — Drew — empathetic not objective — wea[?]
w Woolman's.
commenting on
To P. 30 — I want to see
Furnace fire m[?]
To 57. — John W. a sinner — but what. —
generalizes Spiritual conflict.
mention of Satan P. 55, Voices —
good + bad.
We all compromise — 52
58 — Hannah White — to young woman to
beware of unspiritual young men.
P. 61 + 62 — why resonate to certain
persons + places! — Yes. Phyllis,
Glyndon, Terry[?], chapel, rocking
chair.
66. — liked Indians + Moravian preacher
68 — Nice mention " "

Movings
of
Divine Love

*The Love of God in the Letters of
John Woolman*

Drew Lawson

Inner Light Books
San Francisco, California

2020

Movings of Divine Love
The Love of God in the Letters of
John Woolman

Editor: Charles Martin
Copy editor: Kathy McKay
Layout and design: Matt Kelsey

Published by Inner Light Books

San Francisco, California

www.innerlightbooks.com

editor@innerlightbooks.com

Library of Congress Control Number: 2020946286

ISBN 978-1-7346300-3-9 (hardcover)
ISBN 978-1-7346300-4-6 (paperback)
ISBN 978-1-7346300-5-3 (eBook)

For Fi

who sits beside me
in the garden of Heaven

Contents

John Woolman's Foundation

almighty, divine being, supreme being, divine charity, the Lord Jesus Christ, love of Christ, the simplicity that is in Christ, the wisdom of Christ, the true cornerstone, the creator, the deliverer, the eternal, gracious father, heavenly father, divine fortitude, allsufficiency of God, he who is perfect, goodness, divine hand, never failing portion of happiness, divine help, the great friend and helper, he is a stronghold, glorious in holiness, purity of his judgments, that spirit which suffers long and is kind, Christ our leader, the bread and water of life, pure light, Lord, divine love, heavenly love, movings of divine love, divine majesty, father of mercies, infinite mercies, a love cloaths my mind, thy power, his internal presence, the great preserver, a counceler and safe protecter, divine protection, wise providence, redeemer, refiner, the great shepherd of the sheep, heavenly shepherd, the true shepherd, I feel a pure and holy spirit, divine teacher, him who is able to help through all troubles, truth, the pure light of truth, spirit of truth, a gracious God governs the universe, him who made and commands the winds and the waters, infinite wisdom, pure wisdom, all wise

Words for and about God found in John Woolman's letters

Greetings, Dear Reader

After this manuscript was written in 2000, it languished on the shelves of a bookcase in my office for many years. A number of attempts at getting it published were unsuccessful, and I resigned myself to this never happening. A number of years ago, needing to create space in my office, I discarded many files, including my handwritten notes that identified where I had found each of John Woolman's original letters.

Transforming this material into the book you are reading is due to the herculean efforts of Charles Martin at Inner Light Books and his marvelous copy editor, Kathy McKay. Kathy has found published copies of most of Woolman's letters that I transcribed. However, in some cases published versions of these letters have been edited. Occasionally, I felt the omitted text contributed to the sense of Woodman's relationship with his Quaker community. In those cases, I included the omitted text in this work based on my transcriptions of the text in the original letters and have indicated this with square brackets.

Spending time in the Quaker collections at Haverford College, Swarthmore College, the Historical Society of Pennsylvania, the Library Company (Philadelphia), and Friends House Library in London was a truly wonderful experience. I felt myself enveloped and nurtured by our living Quaker history. Despite being far from home I had much fun and made deep and lasting friendships. I was blessed in so many ways.

May this work encourage you to reflect on your own spiritual journey and deepen your awareness of your relationship with the Divine.

in love and peace,
Drew Lawson
The Whipstick Forest, rural Victoria, Australia, October 2020

Meeting John Woolman

John Woolman was born in New Jersey in the Mid-Atlantic Colonies in 1720 and died of smallpox in a suburb of York, England, in 1772. I first met him in a class led by Bill Taber at Pendle Hill in the spring of 1994. In Bill's class we read Phillips Moulton's edition of John Woolman's journal. As I explored other editions of the journal in search of more biographical information, I came across some of his letters in the edition of his journal edited by Amelia Mott Gummere and published in 1922. The journal (a memoir, in our terminology) is polished and consists of three manuscripts. This is not the case with the letters, except perhaps those he copied into his journal or wrote down later from memory. The journal and the letters portrayed to me a person of great inner strength, a mystic who was committed to taking action arising from his mystical union with God. John Woolman was a prophet and a minister and his letters are one of the forms he used to nurture others. I found myself being led to reflect on what his letters had to tell me about the nature of my own spiritual journey. On one of my annual silent retreats, I was shown that part of my poverty is to give away all that has been given to me in the Silence of God's love. Even my intimate ✓ encounters with God are not mine. I share these writings as part of my obedience to a call to live a life of spiritual poverty, in Silence.

The original manuscript of this book was written in the period 1999–2000, and in the years since I had given up any idea that this work would ever be published. I discarded my original research notes long ago. Apart from the letter to Susannah Lightfoot, I read all of the original letters written in John Woolman's hand. The vast majority of these letters are

iii

held in the Quaker collections at Swarthmore and Haverford Colleges in Pennsylvania. I found two copies of his letter to Susannah Lightfoot – ten pages of handwritten foolscap with only one word different in the two copies, a word that did not affect the meaning. One copy is in the library of Friends House, London. I also found material in the Historical Society of Pennsylvania and the Library Company, Philadelphia. I have no surviving record of the location of any other individual letter. For this book, I have identified published sources for almost all of the letters and other written materials I originally viewed in John Woolman's handwriting. These sources are provided in the endnotes.

Through his words, John Woolman places challenges before me in the light of God's call to me. I write as a pilgrim with a passion for God's wisdom and the wisdom of the saints and an abiding fascination with the patterns of the spiritual path.

Thomas Merton wrote:

> If you want to identify me, ask me not where I live, or what I like to eat, or how I comb my hair, but ask me what I think I am living for, in detail, and ask me what I think is keeping me from living fully the thing I want to live for.[1]

For me, John Woolman is someone for whom the gap between what he professed and how he lived his life is much smaller than for the vast majority of us. I think of John Woolman as the brother of Francis of Assisi. Merton defined a saint as someone who is overwhelmed by the holiness of God. John Woolman is such a saint.

I am embarrassingly aware of the gap between what I profess and the way I live my life. I desire to be overwhelmed by the holiness of God, and though I believe we are all called to that, there are parts of me that still resist. But the life of John Woolman shows me that it is possible to live closer to my profession than I currently do. I believe that as God led John Woolman to this place of faithfulness, God can also lead me (and all of us) if I will allow God to love me that much.

In the past few years, God has moved me far from where I started. In this process, I have constantly found my life catching up to my experience of God; then, God leads me further into the unknown. The gap narrows and expands, narrows and expands. I imagine it will be ever so.

On a silent retreat a few years ago, I had a prayer experience in which John Woolman presented me with his hat. It took me a long time to understand that this was an invitation to a deeper faith in God's love.

John Woolman's ministry was founded on his relationship with God and his wife Sarah's relationship with God and the love they had for each other. It was nourished by his family relationships and the wisdom of friends in his faith community.

This is also true for me. I have learned so much about God's love through the love of my wife, Fiona. Her love helps me to grow and sustains me in the dark times. I am also very blessed to have wise friends to counsel me and hold me in their prayers. The religious life, for me, is meant to be lived in community, and I offer prayers of thanksgiving for the members of my faith community who give me so much love and to friends here in Australia, in the United Kingdom, and in the United States of America and many other places.

All of John Woolman's writings — journal, pamphlets, and letters — issued from a life lived deeply within the culture of the Religious Society of Friends in the eighteenth-century Atlantic colonies. This was a culture steeped in the Christian tradition, steeped in Scripture, steeped in a life lived within a faith community and in a deep understanding of Quaker ways and what it meant to be a Quaker.

John Woolman was committed to the life of his faith community. He was immersed in the sacred texts of the Bible and in the young, one-hundred-year-old tradition of the Religious Society of Friends.

Under the guidance of the Holy Spirit, John Woolman helped give our inheritance a new life and an original expression – and that is why his writings are still of great interest to Friends and the wider faith community.

John Woolman's words describe the eternal in ordinary events and resonate across time.

This book makes available many of the letters of John Woolman and my reflections on themes arising from his letters as I see them in the light of my own experience of the spiritual journey. I write under the banners of the following themes: the love of God, brokenness, abandonment to God, being led through God's love, crucifixion (paying the price of faithfulness), and resurrection. John Woolman was steeped in the Christian tradition, and my approach follows from my own experience of being led on the Christian path.

Brief biographical notes on the lives of John Woolman and of Sarah Woolman are followed by comments on John Woolman's letter-writing ministry. A chapter on a particular theme, with examples from John Woolman's letters, alternates with chapters made up of his letters, allowing readers to hear his voice and have their own response.

John Woolman's letters raise questions on how we listen to a voice from the past, a voice steeped in the Love of God. How do we interpret words written from the Silence?

There are two fundamental questions we all need to address in our journey home to God.

Do we take the love of God seriously?
Will we allow God to love us?

John Woolman could answer both of those questions with a Yes!

May we be inspired to a similar state of openness.

John Woolman: Biographical Note

John Woolman was born on October 19, 1720, at Rancocas, Burlington County, New Jersey. He had six sisters and six brothers. His parents raised their family "to cherish in us a spirit of tenderness, not only toward poor people, but also towards all creatures of which we had the command."[1]

Native Americans and enslaved Africans lived around him. During his early years, approximately 20 percent of the local community owned slaves, including his grandfather. Amelia Mott Gummere, in 1922, characterized Rancocas Meeting and the community in which Woolman dwelt as among the most conservative Quaker enclaves in America at the time.

Woolman became a tailor, part-time orchard keeper, and travelling minister. The first of his many religious journeys took place in 1743.

John Woolman and Sarah Ellis were married in 1749. In 1750 their daughter Mary was born and in 1753 their son, William, who lived but a few months.

In 1754 Woolman's essay "Some Considerations on the Keeping of Negroes" was published and was widely distributed, and it greatly contributed to the declaration against slavery made by Philadelphia Yearly Meeting in 1755. This was the first of a number of essays Woolman wrote.

About 1756 Woolman started composing his journal. He revised it about 1770–1772, and it was first published two years after his death in 1774. Considered a spiritual classic, it has remained continuously in print.

In 1772 Woolman travelled in the ministry to England, and he died in the suburbs of York on October 7, 1772.

John Townsend of London wrote to Sarah Woolman on the death of her husband.

Dear Friend Woolman

Feeling my mind drawn towards thee in near love and tender sympathy for thy great loss of so near a bosom friend thy dear husband. The church's loss is great for which the hearts of many are deeply affected and mourn. But thine and children's loss is much greater. I trust and believe that gracious hand which called him forth into the harvest field will sanctify and sweeten this bitter cup of which thou now hast to drink even to the fulfilling of that gracious promise that all shall work together for good to those who love and fear God.

He lodged at my house when in London. His company and self-denying example were truly profitable to me and family. I doubt not but he has gone to reap the reward of the faithful labourer who loved not the world but was made truly willing to lay down his life in his heavenly master's cause, in that he might be made helpful to any poor soul or souls.[2]

On October 13, 1772, the *Leeds Mercury* reported,

DIED, on Wednesday last, at York, of the smallpox, JOHN WOOLMAN, of New Jersey, in North America, an eminent preacher amongst the people called Quakers. His life exhibited a very singular, and striking example of self-denial; adorned with an amiable sweetness of disposition, and affectionate good will to mankind universally.

His feelings for the bondage and oppression of the poor enslaved negroes, were so exquisite, that he conscientiously refused every accommodation, both in diet and apparel, which was produced by their labour. He was upon a religious visit to his friends in this nation, and has left a wife and family in America.[3]

John Woolman was torn between his love for his family and his calling to minister to the wider community of Friends. But he was faithful to God's call and acted when under a movement of the spirit from our loving God. His journal begins, "I have often felt a motion of Love . . ."

John Woolman did not enjoy good health. He was often sickly. The vitality and energy needed for all the invitations God extended to him would have been beyond human strength had his passion and inner resources not been part of the gift God gave him. Part of John Woolman's message to us is to believe that God will give us what we need to undertake God's promptings.

John Woolman is not a mythological figure but a real human being transformed by the love that God offers each of us. Like all of us, he had his areas of brokenness, his areas of blindness, his times of doubt. The era he lived in produced many wise Friends but was far from perfect. John Woolman is not a product of some golden age that we can never recapture. He lived among ordinary human beings with their particular areas of brokenness — just like me, just like you. His life is an example of what is possible when you allow yourself to fall into God.

When on silent retreat in 1999, I was led to pray with the healing of blind Bartimeus in the Gospel of Mark. Christ, having yet again healed this blind pilgrim, asked me, "Tell me what you see." My reflections on John Woolman's letters are what *I* can see.

In my travels with John Woolman, God has transformed my life in ways beyond my imagining. During this time, I have resisted and finally accepted the call to be a spiritual director. I have twice travelled round the world in the search of the letters of John Woolman. In these travels, I have been nurtured and transformed by those dear friends who have supported my ministries.

Walking the streets of Assisi, the spirit of Clare and Francis can still be felt, the fruit of two lives lived in right ordering with God. Handling the letters of John Woolman gives me the same sense of spiritual truth being transmitted over time.

Although I have limited vision, I write from my own experience and understanding. I pray that God will use these words to speak to you in a way particular to your own journey.

Sarah Woolman: Biographical Note

What has been seen as John Woolman's ministry was actually his and his wife Sarah's ministry. What Sarah provided at home in Mount Holly was an essential part of John's ministry. The love that God gave him through Sarah was a fundamental part of his liberation.

Like John, Sarah had indifferent health. John often travelled away from home in response to a movement of the spirit to minister and, always, to learn. He died across the ocean, in England, when travelling in the ministry. His faithfulness and freedom to travel was founded on his faith but also that of Sarah. As John wrote to Sarah in 1772,

> The numerous difficulties attending us in this life are often before me, and I often remember thee with tender desires that the Holy Spirit may be thy leader, and my leader through life, and that at last we may enter into rest.
>
> John Woolman[1]

There is only one surviving letter written by Sarah, and I quote it below in recognition of her unseen contribution to the life and ministry of her beloved husband. The themes in Sarah's letter are similar to those in John's letters, such as humility, intimacy with God, community wisdom and discernment, and reliance on God.

Sarah's letter was written to an unknown recipient about a teenager named John Smith Jr. in January 1776. According to Amelia Mott Gummere, Sarah

> had known "Johny," as his family called him, since his birth, and took alarm when she found the boy was to be

placed where he might feel "worldly ambitions." He [Johny] was the son of John Smith, her husband's friend, and Hannah Logan. John Smith, 2nd, was born in 1761 and was therefore fifteen years old when this letter was written. . . . Sarah Woolman's fears that his prominent social connections, or his ambitions, if educated to the medical profession, might lead the youthful John astray, were groundless. He chose to devote his time to the cultivation of a highly productive farm, thus following the calling that John Woolman had declared led to the best contentment in life.[2]

Sarah Woolman's letter is as follows:

Dear friend

[A] Concern hath rested on my mind in behalf of John Smith Remembring what Inocence his Dear Creator Bestowed upon him and what a Lamentable Case it should be lost or mard for want timely Care or Chusing a trade may be most for his Spiritual advantage rather than worldly profit may his friends and near Relations dwell Deep in their mind before him whose dwelling is on high may you seek to be directed by best wisdom in so waty a matter and have a watchfull Care over this Beloved youth for his Incouragement in ye Blessed way[.] now hath my mind been united In near Love & Simpathy in Behalf of this Dear Child and his wellfare this Inocence may not be Lost [for] want of Scilfull management[.] I Remember Several years past a friend Said in my hearing if he lived to be old anuf was Intended to bee a doctor or a lawyer[.] it Gave me a [undecipherable] and Sorrow fileth my mind lest it may not prove for his Everlasting advantage aspiring after greatness[.] for alass what is this world and ye pleasures here below when Compared with Eternity Choosing that which may keep his mind most free from entanglements of any kind and this youth be Instructed in the paths of virty and have time to read Good Books and Seek after

6

Humility of hart and find acquaintance & acceptance with his Creator[.] The Humble he will teach of his ways and the Meek guide in Judgment which is more to be valued than all ye pleasures this world Can afford which is very aluring to youth[.] I would Just Expres those hints that I may be Clear for you know I am a poor Cretor and have had a humbling Season and believe these remarks Simple[.] but looking toward the winding up of time hear below and that I may not feel anguish of mind if things Should not Succeed well hereafter and I Could not well be Silent Except I rite Something [of] this kind[.] now if he Should Chuse to be a farmer and you Could find a Honnest man would it not be best and his mind more at Liberty and Serean in meditation on divinity & ye Divine being and may he rule whose rite it is and worthy to have room in our harts[.]

I was Informed by a young man Going to rawway John Smith'[s] 2 unkels Samuel S[mith] & William Login Intended he Should be a docter and the youth rather chose be a farmer[.] young man said was Sorry he Should be a doctor & pityed him to this purpose it caused a fresh Concern in my mind and now dear friend if thou Enquire and if there be not a Cause then rather this was Conceled. I hope thou may alow for weakness and a Stammering [tongue].

farewell S[arah] W[oolman]

rather this had a bee comprised in few words[3]

Writing Letters

John Woolman's correspondence involved messages of friendship, advice, thanksgiving, consolation, inspiration, challenge, and reflections on his own inner struggle. They often provided encouragement to persevere, one of the central necessities for the spiritual life.

In John Wolman's letters, we encounter a spontaneity of expression and a person of wide interests ranging from the mystical to the practical. Many of his letters are very beautiful, and some are dull. Ormerod Greenwood wrote this about a letter from John Woolman to Susannah Lightfoot:

> Here, more than anywhere even in the Journal, he reveals the dark night of the soul which he sometimes knew, in phrases that have none of the careful simplicity of the Journal, but pour out in breathless profusion, the more moving from their formless and impetuous flood.[1]

John Woolman, though, also wrote about the price of salted pork.

Writing letters was obviously a way of life for him, and the speed of delivery meant that local communication by letter was very convenient. Unfortunately, there are many years for which no surviving letters have so far been uncovered.

John Woolman was a highly revered minister, and Friends copied his letters to share with others. The letter to Susannah Lightfoot (written after 1764) only survives because it was copied. In fact, several copies were made with only minor variations between them. In his letters, we encounter his power of speaking under the influence of the Spirit and his ability to move others, which was characteristic of his ministry. In friendship, he was able to receive challenges to reflect on his behavior and was able to lovingly challenge others.

As was the culture and habit of ecclesiastical literature of the time, there are many phrases inspired by Scripture and many direct quotes from Scripture. Travelling into the eighteenth century with him, with its different use of language and expression of the faith journey, we encounter a living and lovable friend. We meet him in his brokenness and in his holiness.

Some of the themes in John Woolman's letters are God's love, spiritual friendship, evil, sanctification, wisdom, the desert, mystery, the dark night, abandonment, suffering, pilgrimage, community and individual discernment, poverty and humility, confusion, thanksgiving, brokenness, crucifixion, resurrection, obedience, despair, self-knowledge, temptation, and joy.

It is interesting that there are two different letters to John Smith in which John Woolman acknowledges Smith challenging him (16 April 1760 and 17 June 1760). One of these letters refers to a dream and to John Smith's appearance in the dream and a challenge given. This would appear, from John Woolman's letter, to be no surprise; i.e. they had the type of relationship in which John Smith could speak in a particular way to John Woolman. This was a particular friendship with particular understandings on what it was possible to say to each other.

Susannah Lightfoot of Philadelphia Yearly Meeting was born in Ireland. She served as an acknowledged minister in Ireland and travelled in the ministry to the American colonies in 1760. Lightfoot moved to Pennsylvania in 1764, where she continued serving as a travelling minister. She died in 1781. Lightfoot appears to have been quite prophetic in her ministry. John Woolman was also prophetic, though perhaps more of a priest. Is it any wonder that John Woolman would write such a letter to another such minister? Do we all not tend to communicate in particular ways to colleagues in our areas of ministry? Perhaps with one or two we are willing to expose ourselves most deeply and at greater length. What is it that is elicited from us when we find a like-minded minister? I find myself sharing a wider view of my experience and understandings, and I find myself surprised by God's revelation that is shown to me from the words I am moved to write to another minister. The listening friend elicits from me wisdom I didn't know I had until the moment of writing. This is essential to be an effective minister. We all need someone to whom we can communicate in the manner of John Woolman's letter to Susannah Lightfoot quoted in the next chapter, to hear ourselves speak and to hear the other's response, and we choose someone we respect and who understands the subtleties of our ministry. John Woolman would appear to have had a deep spiritual relationship with Susannah Lightfoot, and the surviving letter, in handwritten copies, is ten foolscap pages long.

Concerned as he was by the treatment of postboys and their horses, John Woolman preferred his letters to be carried from hand to hand until they reached their recipient. This was possible due to the mobility of Friends, many of whom were travelling in the ministry. One of the consequences of this stand was that letters from, and to, him could take some time to reach their destination.

Dearly beloved Wife

My Companion and I are now at Lynn in health about fifteen miles Eastward from Boston.

I have wrote Several letters to thee, Expecting thou will be glad to hear that I am well, and I write the oftener, for that I suppose they may not all come directly to thy hands.[2]

Dear wife

I heard not from home after I left you till two days ago I rec'd thy two letters, one sent by B.A. (?) and other by H.F. [Hannah Foster], which were truly Acceptable to me.[3]

Three Letters

While all of the surviving letters of John Woolman add to our understanding of him and his view of the nature of our journey three of the letters stand as landmarks: the letter to the Ely family after the death of their young son, the long letter written to Susannah Lightfoot summarizing the nature of our spiritual journey, and the very moving account of John Woolman's last words and death written by William Tuke. These three letters are briefly introduced here and are quoted in full in later chapters (titled John Woolman to the Ely Family, 9 May 1744; John Woolman to Susannah Lightfoot, Sometime after 1764; and William Tuke to Reuben Haines, 26 October 1772).

These letters are troubling, challenging, and uplifting.

John Woolman to the Ely family, 9 May 1744. In May of 1744, John Woolman wrote a letter of love to the Ely family on hearing the news that their young child had died. This letter uses difficult language about the nature of death and raises questions about our understanding of God and the way God works in the world; it also raises questions on the adequacy or inadequacy of our language to describe the inner reality of our intimacy with God.

Woolman writes:

God in . . . wise providence has removed from your embraces a hopeful and pleasant child . . .
God has taken from you a son . . .
He who gives has a right to take away . . .[4]

How can we understand this language in the light of Woolman's frequent descriptions of a loving God? Is it possible to describe the mystery of a soul going home to God? Do we ascribe gifts we receive to an act of grace from God? If so, how then do we describe losses, particularly in such a case where we believe that the child is now fully intimate with God? Or, do we believe something else? When a loved one dies, where do they go? Do we believe in the promise of eternal life, or is our last breath a complete ending? What is death? We have a limited human understanding of God and God's intentions. Is it possible that a short life may be more fruitful in the making of heaven on earth than a long life?

In *The Sign of Jonas*, Thomas Merton wrote:

> I used to think it would be a good thing to die young, and die quickly, but now I am beginning to think a long life with much labor and suffering for God would be the greater grace. However *in concreto* the greater grace for each individual is the one God wills for him. If God wills you to die suddenly, that is a greater grace for you than any other death, because it is the one He has chosen, by His love, with all the circumstances of your life and His glory in view.[5]

Do we get caught in the gulf between desiring free will and the consequences of it when a loved one dies? We want to be in a free, adult relationship with God where we can respond to God's call as we desire. But in illness we want God to directly intervene. Would we be willing to give up our free will?

I have no answers and no language that has meaning outside of Silence. When my father died, in July of 1998, I knew he had stayed alive until my wife and I arrived in Scotland and we could see him. I believe that God called him home, and he went willingly after our mutual articulation of love. But my language sounds mechanical and like Woolman's raises more questions than it answers. I can only talk from my own experience of the Silence surrounding my experience of that loss. For whatever reason, I feel that I was given the grace to allow God to transform my pain into a life-giving event that carries me forward into new life. I was given the grace to enter into the mystery of the transformation of my father through death into life. This was not easy. It was painful, and I still miss him. But I also know that he has joined the communion of saints and is able to be with me when I need him. He is, in a real mystical sense, still alive. Do I, like John Woolman, believe that I will meet those I love in paradise after I die? I have no idea. All I know is that when I enter deeply into the Silence, God may bring my father or my deceased grandmother into my presence in order to teach me, to receive the gift that they have personified.

In 1753, nine years after John wrote the Ely family upon the death of their son, John and Sarah Woolman travelled through the same painful experience when their young son died only a few months into this life. However he, or we, care to describe it, surely the central point of the letter to the Ely family is his encouragement to live in hope while in pain, to believe that God will use this agonising event to help fulfill the creation of God's kingdom. We may not know how, but it is our call to faithfulness to act on the assumption that all will be well. It is our call to faithfulness to live out the reality that our God is a loving God. It is within our call to faithfulness to believe in the transformation that leads to eternal life. Do we believe this? Do we desire this?

Our grieving, our suffering, if we allow it, can be transformed into an invitation to allow God to be even more central in our life than was the case before. We are invited to see beyond the material reality into the reality of mystical eternity. This is a life-long journey full of struggle. But it is also joyful, if we will allow that.

John Woolman to Susannah Lightfoot, after 1764. Sometime after 1764 — the date is uncertain — John

Woolman wrote a letter to Susannah Lightfoot. Like Woolman, she had a prophetic ministry. This letter is much longer than his other letters, as the writer acknowledges:

> My dear Friend, I seem to myself to have exceeded the Bounds of a letter already, altho' I have been obliged to confine my thoughts very much, & have sent thee only a short extract of what has presented itself to my Mind, with a considerable share of warmth & sweetness.[6]

And although its length has contributed to doubt over the authorship of this letter, it is not really surprising that he would write a longer letter to a fellow minister with whom he feels a strong sense of connection.

The topics of the letter include

God's love	spiritual friendship
evil	wisdom
desert	mystery
dark night	abandonment
suffering	pilgrimage
poverty and humility	confusion
brokenness	crucifixion
resurrection	obedience
self-knowledge	temptation
despair	joy

These words contain within them the invitation to hear God's challenge to our own way of being: words of wisdom that travel across time.

William Tuke to Reuben Haines, 26 October 1772. On October 7, 1772, in the suburbs of York, England, John Woolman died in the house of Thomas Priestman. John Woolman was nursed by many Friends, particularly Esther Tuke. The words of the sick man were recorded and incorporated into a letter that William Tuke, Esther's husband, wrote to John Woolman's cousin Reuben Haines later in the month. Tuke describes John Woolman's illness and his journey home to God.

What would we like to be able to say at the end of our life? How would we like to be able to view our life? In our last days, do we desire to say, with John Woolman, "I believe my being here is in the wisdom of Christ?"[7]

John Woolman to the Ely Family, 9 May 1744

Dear Friends,

I have this morning received the melancholy news that God in [undecipherable] and wise providence has removed from your embraces a hopeful and pleasant child by death.

Forgive me dear friends if I inform you that your sorrows on this action find a near avenue to my breast, for 'tis indeed with a tender sympathy I feel your sorrows and share your grief. The wounds and agonies that seize a parents heart on such an occasion can't be thoroughly communicated to one who never felt them, or ever be forgotten by one who has had so long a share in them as I have had.

So that nature as well as Christian duty leads me to mourn with you that weep. God hast taken from you a son in the beginning of the bloom of life: whose sweetness of temper with a complication of desirable endowments of nature, crowned with a virtuous and pious turn of mind seemed to promise much comfort to you and a blessing to the church of Christ in days to come.

But now, alas, the smiles of the morning sun are obscured by dark clouds. The curtains of midnight and the shadows of death overspreads your tabernacle. Your dwelling where the voice of joy and praise has been heard, and the candle of the Lord shined bright, now sits in mourning.

You perhaps are now ready to forget your prosperity and to say as Job did 29th chapter from the 1 pt. to the 6th verse. But dear friends, tho' this be the voice of animal nature and Christianity don't forbid us to give a due vent to our sorrows, yet let us by no means indulge them too far. Let us ascribe righteousness to our maker even when clouds and thick darkness are round about him. He who gives has a right to take away and we ought in humility to bless His holy name. Blessed be God that you are not of the number of those who mourn without hope. Your child, tho' parted from you for a season, you may (I believe) justly hope to meet hereafter in the shining realms of paradise where there is no more death, sorrow nor crying nor any more pain. Where fathers shall not hope in vain nor mothers bring forth for trouble. Those who inhabit there are the blessed of the Lord and their offspring with them.

And now dear friends, what are all the afflictions and sorrows of time when compared with the succeeding [undecipherable] which Christ has purchased for all those that Love him.

I make no doubt but that in this day of your adversity the world and the glories of it appear more empty and vain that they were wont to do in times of prosperity. And probably God may sometimes take away our dearest enjoyments and to teach us to place our highest felicity, content and satisfaction in Himself who is a never failing portion of happiness to all that sincerely trust in Him.

May God sanctify this heavy dispensation of his providence to you and yours for this happy end and while the streams of worldly comforts fail may you be effectually satiated and refreshed with the pure water of the River of Life. May the eternal God be your refuge and underneath may be the everlasting arms. May we so conduct ourselves while we are passing through the pilgrimage assigned us in the wilderness of this world that we may at last through Grace enter into the heavenly [undecipherable] of rest, to the eternal praise of God the Father, Son and Holy Spirit to whom be glory and praise world without end.

So wishes your sincere friend and humble servant J.W.[1]

The Rigorous Logic of Love

The life of John Woolman is an emphatic Yes! to the love offered by God. In his letters and his journal, he is full of God's love for him, God's faithfulness to him, and his faithfulness to God. His relationship with God is an embodiment of the ceiling of the Sistine Chapel where human beings and God reach out to each other.

> [M]any look at the example one of another and too much neglect the pure feeling of truth. Of late years a deep exercise hath attended my mind that Friends may dig deep, may carefully cast forth the loose matter and get down to the rock, the sure foundation, and there hearken to that divine voice which gives a clear and certain sound.[1]

We are invited to make the love of God our rock, the foundation of our existence. The love of God elicits responses from us, responses that are not laid upon us but are in fact our heartfelt desires that are brought to the surface. For we do know, in our soul, what is life-giving for us.

Receiving the love of God elicits our love for God and for all of God's creation. Surfacing from ourselves, we acknowledge our brokenness, our compulsions, and our inner falsities. At this point, healing begins and leads to a desire to follow wherever God leads, at whatever cost. And we are invited to live in hope.

As John Woolman travelled in the ministry, he wrote many letters home to his wife Sarah and daughter Mary. At the end of each letter, without exception, he encouraged them to rely on God and believe in God's love for them.

I recommend you to the Almighty, who I trust cares for you, and under a Sence of his Heavenly Love, remain thy Loving Husband, J. W.[2]

A Good and Gracious GOD Governs the Universe.[3]

The purpose of life is to travel home to God, a process facilitated by God. God invites us and waits for us. God's loving patience is unconditional and always life-giving. As God invited us into the flesh, out of Love, so does God invite us into the eternal, out of Love. Thomas Merton describes this in his own life:

> The happiness that is so pure because it is simply not one's own making but sheer mercy and gift. Happiness in the sense of having arrived at last in the place destined for me by God; of fulfilling the purpose for which I was brought here.[4]

We are born blessed, with an unconscious awareness living in our soul of who God made us to be. But we enter a society full of brokenness with which we cooperate in many ways and allow ourselves to be diverted from our holy path. So, in a very real sense, spiritual formation is about being re-formed into who we essentially are. And it is the love of God that forms us if we will be attentive.

In a letter written in late 1756, John Woolman compares our formation to that of minerals in a furnace. We are formed by the fire of God's love, a love that will not give us more than we can bear, whose actions always lead to clarity and new life. God desires to transform us, to strengthen us so that we can stand against the evil spirit which leads us from the path of our true beingness.

> In this thy late affliction I've found a deep fellow-feeling with thee, and had a secret hope throughout that it might please the Father of Mercies to raise thee up & sanctifie thy troubles to thee, that thou being more fully

20

acquainted with that way which the world esteems foolish may feel the Cloathing of Divine Fortitude, and be strengthened to Resist that spirit which leads from the Simplicity of the Everlasting Truth.[5]

Turning our hearts over to God so that God's will and our will are indistinguishable is, as John Woolman says, like the purification that takes place in a furnace. And although the furnace from the outside may seem just a one-step process, it is far from that; the process of total abandonment to God is the work of a lifetime.

Subjecting our will to that of God, allowing God to transform our will to God's will, and turning our hearts over to God so that God's will and our will are indistinguishable is no easy thing. The minerals are added to the furnace. They are not hot, and they are not homogeneous; they are a collection of unconnected, independent elements. The minerals start to warm, and then they start to melt. Edges begin to blur. As they become more fluid and hotter, amalgamations start to happen. What were separate start to come together. Slag starts to form on the surface. At the exit of the furnace, the slag is taken off. The new material, almost totally homogeneous, flows from the body of the furnace.

But first we have to decide whether we want to get closer to God. *Listen!* says the Lord, *I am standing and knocking at your door* (Revelation 3:20 CEV). The invitation is there. God is patiently, lovingly waiting. God will not force us. We have to exert our will, express our desire. Having opened the door, God comes closer, the Light gets brighter, the presence of the Holy Spirit becomes stronger, and the touch of Christ is firmer.

We have walked into the rose garden, and we are people at war with ourselves but searching for peace. There are many parts of us: the parts we think are gifts, the parts we think are death-giving; those parts of us that we know we are avoiding;

and the major part of ourselves that we didn't know was there — our God-given giftedness that is beyond our wildest imaginings. How often have we thought, "It would be great to be like . . . "? What a lowly ambition — for God has something better planned for us: ourselves.

Like all purification processes, there are many furnaces to travel through. At each stage the slag, the light, insubstantial waste, is drawn off, leaving the deeper, richer *us* flowing from the body of Christ. The person emerging from God's furnace has cast off their unnecessary burdens and has become integrated with themselves and God and has become that great gift to God's creation — the person God made them to be. Nothing less, nothing more.

We will still contain some degrees of nonhomogeneity, some degree of brokenness, but that is the nature of the human condition. God is always offering us more, always holding out Her healing hand; there is always more even until our final breath: *always more.*

The underpinning all of this journey is the Truth that God loves each of us unconditionally.

I pray that this "melting operation of the hand of God,"[6] as John Woolman put it in one of his letters, does indeed become a necessity, that it becomes a choice that is a nonchoice for we know that we can do no other. May our hearts long with a deep longing for the fire of God that leads to new life.

> As soon as I believed that there was a God I understood that I could do nothing but live for Him alone.
>
> Charles de Foucauld to Henri de Castries[7]

This fire is an invitation to live immersed in God, to turn away from all that is not of God. It is an invitation to step out on that life-giving but most difficult journey of taking each step with God, of realizing that each breath comes from God and that every part of every moment becomes imbued with God. It is a journey undertaken with a Heart (mind and heart together) permanently available to God, with the door to the rose garden always open.

The fire elicits from us a deep love of God and a desire to serve God and to follow wherever God leads. The consolation of a life lived with God may at times be very difficult, may contain dark nights of the soul. We may even be led to the point of death, and our attachment to earthly things may be greatly loosened. God opens our eyes, and we take another step along the path that leads into total communion with God for we realize the temporary nature of earthly things in a new way. We realize that our Heart belongs with God — the dark night, the dry desert, the point of death all give us life by bringing us closer to God.

The following is from my 1994 retreat journal:

> I am presented with an image of a box. It is full. Wrapped in tissue paper are all the precious gifts God has given me. Nothing more can be fitted into the box. It is marvelous to look at. I feel very blessed, and unsuspecting, for I feel that this image has been given to signify the end of the retreat. Instead, I am presented with a beginning, not an ending. *Talk to God!*

> "Look at all the gifts I have given you Drew. There is something you have not seen yet. There is something more, right in the centre of the box, look closely."

> Putting my eyes very close I can just make out there is a small gap right in the middle of all these gifts. I step inside and find myself in a desert. At first it feels very pleasant, a nice sunny day. Slowly I realise that there is nothing growing, there are no clouds in the sky, no birds, no animals at all, no water. Finally I become aware I have no idea which direction to move in and I

have no sense at all of God's presence. I feel lost, alone, desolate, confused.

"If you want this box you must accept everything that is in it. The desert comes with the gifts. If you accept the box you accept the desert too."

There are times in our journey when such an intensity of experience is necessary to remove another set of veils from our eyes. John Woolman wrote:

I believe our afflictions are often permitted by our heavenly Father for our more full and perfect refining.

The Truth my dear sister, hath been precious in thy sight and I trust remains to be to thee precious as ever.

In the pure and undefiled way, that which is not of the Father, but of the world, is purged out.[8]

God's love elicits from us a concern for others. Central to the Christian call is the invitation to be in relationship with God, with Christ, with the Holy Spirit, with ourselves, and with each other; this is fundamental. From this well of concern, John Woolman writes many of his letters. As with Sarah, he encourages others to have faith in God's love.

There is a love Cloaths my mind while I write, which is superior to all Expressions, & I find my heart open to encourage to a holy Emulation to advance forward in Christian firmness.[9]

As Woolman travelled in the ministry and encountered inner and outer difficulties, he experienced God's love for him, a love that called forth his love for others.

He [the Lord] regards the helpless and distressed, and reveals his Love to His Children under Affliction, they delight in beholding his Benevolence, & feeling Divine Charity moving upon them: Of this I may speak a little, for though since I left you, I have often found an Engaging love & Affection towards thee and my daughter, and Friends about home.[10]

A pivotal and life-changing grace that John Woolman allowed himself to receive was the knowledge that he was lovable: loved by God, loved by Sarah, loved by friends. Arising from his own recognition and reception of God's unconditional love for him, through others and directly from God, was the depth of his love for others.

Both of these states he acknowledges in his letters.

From letters to Sarah:

> I have wrote Several letters to thee, Expecting thou will be glad to hear that I am well, and I write the oftener, for that I suppose they may not all come directly to thy hands. . . .

> I remember thee and my child often with much nearness of Affection, believing thou art Somewhat lonesome in my Absence, and the most comfortable thoughts I have on the Subjects are That a Good and Gracious GOD governs the Universe, who makes all things work for good to them that love him, of which number I trust thou art one.

> My love is to my dear Fr'ds. about home.[11]

> Dear wife

> I heard not from home after I left you till two days ago I rec'd thy two letters one Sent by B.A. (?) & other by H.F. [Hannah Foster], which were truly Acceptable to me.

> I hear by Wm. Lightfoot thou hast been poorly but at the time of his passing by was better. Thy not mentioning it in thy letters, I consider as intended kindness to me by forbearing to contribute to the Increase of my Exercise. I feel a most tender Concern

for thee, as knowing thy Condition to be Attended with dificulty, and find at times a disposition to hasten for thy Sake. . . .

My Care about thee and my Child is much greater than any other Care (as to the Things of this life) but my comfort hath all along been that a Greater than I is careful for you, to whose Gracious protection I recommend you.[12]

And again:

Dear wife

I rec'd thy two letters at Newport dated the 19: and 20: of the mo. 5 and how acceptable they were to me is not Easie to Express.[13]

Sarah's letters had taken over a month to reach him.

The deeper the relationship with God, the more a life of faithfulness is elicited from a person. The Spirit is patient with us and suffers with us when we are stuck in our pain and is always leading us to a life-giving way. John Woolman willingly bathes in the river of God's love and relies on, experiences, and is obedient to God's presence in the midst of his trials. Woolman's experience of God on his travels is Goodness. God is the rock to hang on to in time of trouble — not as a last resort but a first resort. God is faithful; God helps those who humbly trust in him.

My life from one minute to another is Sustained by him,
All I have are his gifts, and I am endeavouring (though in weakness) to Surrender all to him.[14]

[Y]et through the Mercy of the Almighty I am enabled to persue our Journey.[15]

To Him who is a Father, a counceler and safe protecter to His family. Through the various deficulties which attend them in this world, I recomend thee and my beloved friend thy companion.[16]

John Woolman has a deep faith in Divine providence. In a letter to Sarah, he writes:

That Pure Light which enlightens every man coming into the World to me appears as Lovely as Ever. To the guidance of which I hope thee and I may Attend while we live in this world, and then all will be well.[17]

To John and Mary Comfort (his daughter and son-in-law) he emphasizes that God will support them if they will pay attention and allow it. He has great faith in God assisting us in our afflictions. Many people only turn to God when they are well and can give God good news. But God is with us in our pain and cries with us, is particularly close to us in these times, and longs to hear our cries of supplication.

Dear Children:

I feel a tender care for you at this time of parting from you, and under this care, my mind is turned toward the pure Light of Truth, to which if you take diligent heed I trust you will find inward Support under all your trials.

My leaving you under the trying Circumstances now attending you, is not without close exercise and I feel a living concern, that under these cares of business, and under bodily affliction, your minds may be brought to a humble waiting on Him who is the great Preserver of his people. Your loving parent

John Woolman.[18]

Embracing the Love of God leads to an uplifting of the Spirit, a sense of lightness, and a clarity of vision. From the depths of silence each blade of grass vibrates with life, bird song resonates in new ways, and a wave of love seems to flow outwards, powered by the Holy Spirit. John Woolman calls this state one of freedom.

> I feel that pure love toward thee in which there is freedom.[19]

In his letter to Susannah Lightfoot (written sometime after 1764), he brings together many of his themes on the love of God. We know each other through communion with God and become one body in a mysterious way that the world does not recognise. When we are in a loving state, our friend's joy is our joy and our friend's pain is our pain. God is always present to help us. Will we make ourselves available to God?

Our journey teaches us to recognise that God gives us what we need (rather than what we want). As God becomes more and more the centre of our lives, we grow into discipleship. And, like Jesus' disciples, our lives are full of miracles. We will see them if we pay attention.

God is more hopeful for us, individually and collectively, than we are. God only calls us to whatever we can do and only gives us the amount of Love we can bear at that time. God's knowledge of us is greater than ours, and God knows we are stronger and more gifted than we think we are.

> So, let us trust in God. Let us trust in The most Gracious and most tender Visitations of Christ to our Souls.[20]

The following is from my 1999 retreat journal on praying with the healing of Bartimaeus in the Gospel of Mark.

> Jesus is calling me. Jesus wants me to be closer to Him. I am full of joy, and expectation and peace. After throwing off my cloak Jesus asks me what I want.
>
> "I want to see again."

28

"You have flung off your cloak, the cloak of your blindness, you can see. Tell me what you see."

N "I see a beautiful world, full of potential and possibilities. I see a world bathed in the love of God. I see hope everywhere."

Thomas Merton writes:

This is a gift of God marked with His simplicity and His purity. How one's heart opens and what hope arises in the core of my being! It is as if I had not really hoped in God for years, as if I had been living all this time in despair.

Now all things seem reasonable and possible. . . . A whole new dimension of life is no longer a desperate dream but completely and simply credible.

Thomas Merton, *A Vow of Conversation*[21]

The rigorous logic of love. ✔

Letters: February 1755 to December 1760

25 February 1755, to Catherine Payton of Dudley

Beloved Friend C. Payton

I thought I wanted some more conversation with thee than I had opertunity for.

Haveing been at Sunday Meetings with thee I perceive that He who waits to be gracious to us has given thee among others a distinct sight of the state of the Churches. To Him only I am thankfull for it.

And from a warm desire that thy clearness of understanding may be continued, missing other means take this to remind thee of what thou well knowest. That where the Divine hand bestow liberally deep reverence is more abundantly necesary.

And if thou keepest near enough the centre of humility, I think I see a blessing to us will ensue –

In much haste and fine love

I am thy friend   John Woolman[1]

21 June 1755, to John Smith

Esteemed Friend

John Smith

One of Wm. Sheeveres Sons (a young man with a wife and small children), having been lunatick, I believe, near a year — his wife was lately speaking to me to write a paper for a neighbour to sign in order to introduce him into your hospital.

I not knowing whither he would be received or not if so recommended chose to write to thee first (as thou I expect has some knowledge of the family and the state of the hospital).

At present the young people live with their parents. Their father has long been troubled with the like disorder — and is incapable of much business.

Their mother has an ulcer on one leg by which she is quite helpless and thought to be incurable without cutting off, which she, considering her age, does not think proper.

Their neighbours are kind and I expect will be —

It's their doctor has proposed to them the hospital.

> Thy answer for their sake will
> be acceptable to thy friend
> John Woolman[2]

Late 1756, to an unknown recipient, perhaps one of the Pemberton brothers or John Smith

In this thy late affliction I've found a deep fellow-feeling with thee, and had a secret hope throughout that it might please the Father of Mercies to raise thee up & Sanctifie thy troubles to thee, that thou being more fully acquainted with that way which the world esteems foolish may feel the Cloathing of Divine Fortitude, and be strengthened to resist that spirit which leads from the Simplicity of the Everlasting Truth.

We may see ourselves cripled and halting, & from a strong bias to things pleasant and easie, find an Impossibility to advance forward: but things Impossible with men are possible with God; and our wills being made Subject to his, all temptations are Surmountable.

This work of Subjecting the will, is compared to the mineral in the furnace, which through fervent heat is

31

reduced from its first principle. "He refines them as silver is refined; He shall sit as a refiner and purifier of silver." By these Comparisons we are instructed in the necessity of the melting operation of the hand of God upon us, to prepare our hearts truly to adore Him, and manifest that adoration by inwardly turning away from that Spirit in all its workings which is not of Him. To forward this work, the allwise God is sometimes pleased, through outward distress, to bring us near the gates of Death; That life being painful & afflicting, and the prospect of Eternity open before us, all earthly bonds may be loosened, and the mind prepared for that deep and Sacred Enstruction, which otherwise would not be received.

If kind parents love their children and delight in their happiness, then He who is perfect goodness in sending abroad mortal Contagions, doth Assuredly direct their use. Are the righteous removed by it? their change is hapy: Are the wicked taken away in their wickedness? the Almighty is clear. Do we pass through it with anguish and great bitterness, & yet recover? he intends that we should be purged from dross, and our ear opened to discipline.

And now on thy part, after thy Sore Affliction and doubts of recovery, thou art again restored, forget not Him who hath helped thee, but in humble gratitude hold fast his instructions, thereby to shun those by paths which leads from the firm foundation. I am Sensible of that variety of Company, to which one in thy business must be Exposed. I have painfully felt the force of conversation proceeding from men deeply rooted in an Earthly mind, and can sympathize with others in Such Conflicts, in that much weakness still attends me. I find that to be a fool as to worldly wisdom, & commit my cause to God not fearing to offend men who take offence at the Simplicity of Truth, is the only way to remain unmoved at the Sentiments of others.

The fear of man brings a snare: by halting in our duty, & giveing back in the time of tryal, our hands grow weaker, our Spirits get mingled with the people, our ears grow dull as to hearing the language of the True Shepherd; that when we look at the way of the Righteous, it seems as though it was not for us to follow them.

There is a love Cloaths my mind while I write, which is superior to all Expressions, & I find my heart open to encourage to a holy emulation to advance forward in Christian firmness. Deep Humility is a strong bulwark; & as we enter into it, we find safety and true Exaltation: The foolishness of God is wiser than man, and the weakness of God is Stronger than man. Being uncloathed of our own wisdom, and knowing the Abasement of the creature, therein we find that power to arise, which gives health and Vigor to us.

John Woolman.[3]

1 October 1757, to Abraham Farrington

Dear Friend,

Thine from Liverpool to J. White and me, came to hand, of which I was glad, and intended to return answer soon, but in the Spring was prevented by an embargo, — the fore part of the Summer was in Virginia and Carolina, and since my return till now have had no agreeable opportunity.

[Jose was pretty well yesterday, I see him often at meetings - weekdays as well as other days. I had some conversation with Mary at out Yearly Meeting, she being then in Philadelphia. I think she is in the way of mending. Samuel is much at his mill. He keeps a trunk at my house and when in town is pretty often on that account to see me. He was well when I heard from him last.]

I may say with thankfulness that the kindness of Providence is still near to his people, to give counsel in times of distress and difficulty. The need we have of His help some of late have been more sensible [of] than heretofore.

After raising 1000 men in this Province by a draft of the Militia, to go out on an emergency, was fresh orders in our county to draft three times that number, to hold themselves in readiness to march at any time when called upon. In this second draft several young men of our Society were chosen. On the day appointed to meet the captain, in our town, several of our young men, not less than four or five, came and acquainted him in substance as follows: that for conscience sake they could not fight, nor hire any one to go in their stead, and that they should not go out of his way. They were all dismissed at that time with orders to remain in readiness, and soon after there came account from the general that they were not likely to want them this time. It was a day of deep trial to the young men, yet the effect it appeared to have on their minds was such, that I thought I saw the kindness of Providence in it, and trust that if it should please Him to try us with further and heavier sufferings than what we have yet had, his arm will be sufficient to uphold them who really trust in Him. In the first draft I know not of any of our young men in town being drafted, but in some places they were, and to such who stood true to their principles, tho' they were taken away and nearly tried, I have not heard that the officers were inclining to severity.

[Dear Thomas Brown is deceased, also Caleb Haines, Barzillai Newbold, Patrick Reynolds, John Hilliard, E. Hopkins, Mary Smith, etc. At our Yearly Meeting we had the company of Samuel Spavold, Thomas Gawthrop, Christopher Wilson, John Hunt, William Reckitt, Benjamin Ferris, also Thomas Nicholson, from Carolina. The great goodness was near us. James Tasker was this day at my house on return from New England. Samuel Spavold is now going, as I understand, to Carolina.

Our late governor died about three weeks past and John Reading at present succeeds in the administration.]

There are degrees of growth in the Christian progress, and all well meaning people are not in the same degree entered into that resignation, wherein men are crucified to the world; hence sometimes ariseth a diversity of sentiments in regard to matters of faith and practice. Tho' this be in some measure the case of our Society in regard to paying money raised for the defence of our country, love and charity is however in a good degree preserved. *war Taxes*

Thy friend,

John Woolman[4]

10 September 1758, to John Smith

Belovd Friend

John Smith

Our Friend Esther Andrews departed this life about 8 o'clock this morning. They propose to bury her corps tomorrow in the afternoon, to meet at the house where she lived at 2 o'clock. If thou would please to mention it in your meeting this afternoon, with a general Invitation to friends, it will be Acceptable to those who have the care of the burial.

thy Loving frd.
John Woolman[5]

16 April 1760 to John Smith

Belov'd Friend

I rec'd that letter from I.P. at a time when my mind was so Employ'd about endeavouring to put my family and affairs in a condition to leave them with satisfaction; And that, with the Shortness of the Time before me, seem'd to make it very difficult for me to do anything in it. And meeting with J. Noble, I saw no better way than to send thee the letter.

I understood the hundrd pound to Mary was to be paid in 3 years after her Father's decease, which is not yet Expir'd. I propos'd to Mary some weeks ago to take a bond of S.A. for that Sum that might be due. She seem'd Easie to have it in Samuel's hands till time of payment as believing it safer, and I was Cautious, as the money was not due, of moveing anything which might beget uneasiness in the family; but if any who are more fully acquainted with his Circumstance, think the Case requires it, I Expect he would let her have £100 in [undecipherable] hands at the request of f'rds. So no more at present as to that.

Last night in my Sleep I thought I was in a Room with thee, and thou drawing thy chair nigh mine, did, in a friendly way, tell me of Sundry particular failings thou had observed in me, and Expressd some desire that I might do better. I felt inwardly thankfull for thy care over me, and made little other reply than to tell thee that I took it very kind.

Allmost as Soon as I awoke I remembered it, and though I could see some things in which I had not done so well as I might, yet the particulars thou pointed out were gone from me, nor can I yet remember them.

I am about to leave home under much thoughtfulness, & at times it seems to border upon distress of Mind. But [I] retain a desire to put my whole trust in Him who is able to help throug [sic] all troubles,

With kind Love to thee and thy wife, I remain your f'rd

John Woolman[6]

16 4 1760

I hope my dear Wife will be noticed by her friends.

J.W.[7]

16 April 1760, to John Pemberton

Dear Friend

The Matter thou mentioned in thy Letter a few days past I had thought a good deal of and talked with Mary about it, but had not seen a clear way to do anything in it.

I rec'd thine on Second day last, and expect to leave home this day; that as Mary is not here now, there was no Opertunity for me to do anything. Especially as I was thoughtful to put my family in a Condition to leave.

As thou mentioned J. Smith as one who might be a Friend to Mary, I knew not how to do better than to Acquaint him with the care thou had on her Account, which I have done, and so with Kind kind (sic) love to thee & thy Mother and Enquiring f'rds, I remain

thy f'rd,

John Woolman.[8]

24 April 1760, to Sarah Woolman

Dearly belovd wife —

We are favoured with health, have been at Sundry meetings in East Jersey & on this Island [Long Island]. My mind hath been in an inward watchfull frame Since I left thee, greatly desiring that our proceedings may be singly in the will of Our Heavenly Father.

As the present appearance of things is not joyous, I have been much shut up from outward Chearfulness, remembering that promise, "Then shalt thou delight thyself in the Lord." As this from day to day has been revived in my memory, I have considered that his Internal presence on our minds is a delight of all others the most pure; and that the honest hearted not only delight in this, but in the Effect of it upon them. He regards the helpless and distressed, and reveals his Love to His Children under Affliction, they delight in beholding his Benevolence, and feeling Divine Charity moving upon them: of this I may speak a little, for though since I left you, I have often found an Engaging love & Affection towards thee and my daughter, and friends about home; that going out at this time, when Sickness is so great amongst you, is a tryal upon me; yet I often remember there are many Widows and Fatherless, many who have poor Tutors, many who have evil Examples before them, and many whose minds are in Captivity, for whose sake my heart is at times moved with Compassion, that I feel my mind resigned to leave you for a Season, to exercise that gift which the Lord hath bestowed on me, which though small compared with some, yet in this I rejoyce, that I feel love unfeigned toward my fellow-creatures. I recommend you to the Almighty, who I trust cares for you, and under a Sence of his Heavenly Love, remain thy Loving Husband, J. W.[9]

11 May 1760, to John Smith

Dear Friend

My Companion and I are now at Newport, and midling well. Was yesterday at the burial of Abram Redwood's Wife, and Expect if favour'd with health & way opens to be at Boston the latter end of the week and to return from the Eastward to Newport Yearly Meeting.

I shall take it kind if thou'll please to take care of the Enclos'd, & should be glad to hear how my dear Wife and Child are, and fr'ds about home, not forgetting the Small pox was brief. (?)

Our Visits in general have hitherto been in weakness, and to me it hath been a time of Abasement. I hope, notwithstanding, our appointing meetings have not been to the dishonour of Truth. My Exercises have, I think, been at least usefull to me, & I am thankfull to the Almighty in that I have seen and felt that He knows best what is for our good, and the good of fr'ds where we come.

In some humbling Seasons, I have thought of my dear f'rds about home, and amongst others, thou and thy wife have been frequent in my remembrance.

John Woolman

fr'ds here are generally well.[10]

18 May 1760, to Sarah Woolman

Dearly beloved Wife

My Companion and I are now at Lynn in health about fifteen miles Eastward from Boston.

I have wrote Several letters to thee, Expecting thou will be glad to hear that I am well, and I write the oftener, for that I suppose they may not all come directly to thy hands.

It would be Agreeable to me to hear from you, not haveing had any Intelligence Concerning you Since I saw you, nor do I expect any soon as I am continually going from home. But should way open for our Journey I hope to be at the further end of it in less than two weeks, and then return toward Newport Yearly Meeting.

I remember thee and my child often with much nearness of affection, believing thou art Somewhat lonesome in my Absence. And the most comfortable thoughts I have on the Subjects are that a Good and Gracious GOD governs the Universe, who makes all things work for good to them that love him, of which number I trust thou art one. My love is to my dear Fr'ds. about home.

John Woolman.[11]

14 June 1760, to Sarah Woolman

Dear wife

I heard not from home after I left you till two days ago I rec'd thy two letters one Sent by B.A. (?) & other by H.F. [Hannah Foster], which were truly Acceptable to me.

I hear by Wm. Lightfoot thou hast been poorly but at the time of his passing by was better. Thy not mentioning it in thy letters, I consider as intended kindness to me by forbearing to contribute to the Increase of my Exercise. I feel a most tender Concern for thee, as knowing thy Condition to be Attended with dificulty, and find at times a disposition to hasten for thy Sake. But Such is the weight of the work I am engaged in, and Such the baptisms with which I have been baptized; that I see A Necessity for all nature to Stand Silent. I know not that I ever have had a Sharper Conflict in Spirit, or better understood what it was to take up the Cross, than of late. The depth of which Exercise is know (sic) only to the Almighty, and yet my beloved companion Saml. [Samuel Eastburn] hath been a true and faithful Sympathizer with me. I am humbly Thankfull to My Gracious Father, who has brought my mind in a good degree to be resigned to him.

From Him my being is derived. My life from one minute to another is Sustained by him, All I have are his gifts, and I am endeavouring (though in weakness) to Surrender all to him. My Care about thee and my Child is much greater than any other Care (as to the Things of this life) but my comfort hath all along been that a Greater than I is careful for you, to whose Gracious protection I recommend you.

The frds. from our parts are all here & appear to be well. We have been generally pretty well, have got forward on our Journey. There remains about 14 meetings besides Nantucket which we have not been at. Should we be favoured to get through them we Expect to go for Oblong in York Governmt.

Spare no cost to make thy life Comfortable as may be. I say so because I heard by H.F. thou wast disappointed about a young woman.

My love is to all my dear frds.

John Woolman.[12]

17 June 1760, to John Smith

Dear fr'd

After I left home I heard not from my family till I came to Newport Yearly Meeting at which I rec'd two letters from thee, dated 18: and 25: 5mo., and how acceptable they were is hard to Express.

Some pt. of thy first and longest letter has had a particular and frequent place in my Consideration, and I think has done me a little good. I was helped with a little help.

The Yearly Meeting is now finish'd. E.S. [Elizabeth Shipley] and H.F. [Hannah Foster] are going to Boston and Eastward. J. Storer expects to visit some Mo. meetings round about N.Y. M.R. [Mary Ridgway], S.E. [Samuel Eastburn] and I Expect to go to Nantucket Yearly Meeting, if way open.

I find no Memorial in any records in this Y. Meeting, but now at this Seting friends have made a Minute in the

Y.M. Book, a Copy to be sent to the Quartrs &c., to do that work.

Thy kindness in sending my letters is gratefully own'd. Truth is the same in all places: it is felt and own'd by Multitudes of people who yet are distinguished by Some Circumstances (some inded of whom do not live up to what they see to be right), and the clearer the discovery, the Stronger the Obligation to labour in that Spirit which Suffers long and is kind, thereby if haply to point out the more perfect way.

I have had to Admire that Wisdom who appoints to his Servants their several and respective Employments: and to Adore that power which hath Supported my Soul and kept me in a resignation through some uncommon Exercises. I remember you often with much nearness, and allsoe my dear fr'ds about home.

John Woolman[13]

17 June 1760, to Abner Woolman

Dear Brother,

I have remembered (since I left home) thee and thy family very often with much nearness of love.

We are at Newport and expect to go for Nantucket soon, if way open. We have been fellow feelers with the afflicted, nor is any affliction too great to endure for the Truth. This I own, and am labouring daily to be found in that resignation.

I am pinched for time, but wanted to let thee know I often thought of you.

John Woolman[14]

23 June 1760, to Sarah Woolman

Dear wife

I rec'd thy two letters at Newport dated the 19: and 20: of the mo. 5 and how acceptable they were to me is not Easie to Express. I wrote from Newport about a week past and Expecting tomorrow if the wind be fair and way open to Sail for Nantucket, was desirous to leave a few lines to be forwarded by any Opertunity.

We have been at five meetings Since the Yearly Meeting and I may say by Experience the Lord is good he is a Strong hold in the day of trouble, and helpeth those who humbly trust in him. E. Shipley and H. Foster are gone for Boston and Eastward A. Gaunt and M.R. [Mary Ridgeway] expect to Sail for Nantucket, J. Storer is in these parts & all midling well. People in these parts are generally favoured with health. I have heard very little of the smallpox since I came of (sic) Long Island.

I am not so hearty and healthy as I have been Sometimes, and yet through the Mercy of the Almighty I am enabled to persue our Journey without much difficulty on that Account.

Every year brings Additional Experience and I think I never more clearly saw the reasonableness and fitness of Casting all my cares on God than I have Since I left thee.

I remember thee and my Child with endeared love and tenderness, knowing how much you miss me.

I remember also that God is wise, he knows what is for the best. He is good and willing to make us as happy, as we are capable of being.

He is strong and nothing is hard for him; that to Love him and Serve him in Sincerity is the best way for us in this world. He is high and Inhabits Eternity, and dwells allso with them that are poor & of a Contrite Spirit. Trust him, my dear, and I fear not thou'l do well.

John Woolman.

I name none of my dear Fr'ds. but my love is to them all.[15]

12 December 1760, to Jane Crosfield

Since I understand thy draft toward New England at this season of the year, I have felt a near sympathy in my mind toward thee, and also thy new companion, H. White.

mom's?

Looking seriously over the stages and wide waters and thinking on the hard frosts and high winds usual in the winter, the journey has appeared difficult; but my mind was turned to him, who made and commands the winds and the waters, and whose providence is over the ravens and the sparrows.

I believed thou understood his language, and I trust thy ear will be attentive to him, and in that there is safety in the greatest difficulties. "He that believeth maketh not haste," and there seemed a hint in my mind to give thee, that thou take a sufficient portion of that doctrine along with thee this journey. Should frozen rivers or high winds or storms sometimes prevent thy going forward so fast as thou could desire, it may be thou may find a service in tarrying even amongst a people whose company may not be every way agreeable. I remembered that the manner in which Paul made a visit to the island of Melita was contrary to his own mind as a man; we find, however, that by means thereof, the father of Publius was healed of his fever, and many cured of their infirmities.

Farewell, my dear Friend.

John Woolman.

12 12, at night, 1760.

The want of a suitable opportunity this evening occasioned me to take this way.[16]

Searching for John Woolman's Dead Kangaroo

I wrote this in my journal about a retreat prayer experience:

> I am standing at the northwest corner of our top paddock. On the other side of the dilapidated fence grows the extended forest. A few trees have strayed over the fence to our side. A utility, driven by young men, roars up the forest side of the fence. It stops, the men jump out and throw a dead kangaroo from the back of the utility into the paddock.

> This part of the paddock is at the top of a very gentle slope that starts near the road on the other side of our front fence.

> From where I am standing, next to the decaying, fly-infested flesh of the kangaroo, the top part of the paddock is clay and small rocks. Fragile grass grows there in good seasons, and beautiful small violet-blue flowers. There is an erosion ditch diagonally across the end of this paddock. Sometimes the water flows, but mostly it is dry. The ditch line is marked by trees.

> On the other side of the ditch the poor land continues for a little way, but next to the road the soil is rich. This is where we have placed the orchard and lots of native trees that sing with pink and red flowers in spring. Very beautiful. Fruit of many kinds.

The dead kangaroo and the flowering gum trees are both part of me and mark my humanness. At one point I thought my whole life was encompassed by the dead kangaroo.

Many of the people I have worked with as a spiritual director have had a tendency only to see the dead kangaroo, have yet to see God with them in their pain. Their inner pain has meant they deny their inherent goodness, creativity, and divinity. Their view of their life, as mine had been, is but a small section of a rich tapestry of which brokenness is a part but not the whole.

This same inner pain has coloured their view of others, particularly those we would call saints. People such as John Woolman become remotely pure and of a standard to which they, as broken people, can never aspire. It seems as if God had zapped John Woolman with a bolt of lightning, but God has not zapped them. They say they are not worthy. Bolt-of-lightning theology undermines the significance of grace and denies the reality of the invitation given to all of us; denies the reality of the need to allow God to transform our brokenness; denies the work required for that, the perseverance; denies the call to be who God made us to be — saints.

As I started reading John Woolman and talking to Friends about John Woolman, I found I was seeing myself next to the flowering grey-box tree, picking ripe fruit from the fig trees, standing in the sun with no cloud or rain. And, I was viewing John Woolman as two-dimensional.

Standing amidst creation God showed me my goodness opposed to my darkness, John Woolman, being human, had his darkness next to his goodness. The addition of his darkness increases his humanity, increases the power of his witness, gives me a real human person to be inspired by.

In my experience, it is through our knowledge of our brokenness that God uses us. We are not ready to be apostles if we cannot name and acknowledge our brokenness for this *is* our Truth and must be stated.

John Woolman knew his brokenness; he knew he was loved by God in his brokenness; he knew God used him in his brokenness; he knew he was an apostle in his brokenness; he knew he did not need to be perfect to be an apostle.

> O Lord! it was thy power that enabled me to forsake Sin in my Youth, and I have felt thy Bruises since for disobedience, but as I bowed under them, thou healedst me; and though I have gone through many Trials and sore Afflictions, thou hast been with me, continuing a Father and a Friend. . . .
>
> . . . My dependence is in the Lord Jesus Christ, who I trust will forgive my Sins, which is all I hope for; and if it be his Will to raise up this Body again I am content; and if to die, I am resigned.[1]

In a letter dated 16 April 1760, John Woolman wrote to his friend John Smith about a dream he had had. Smith was obviously a very close friend of his, someone Woolman saw as having wisdom. God used the image of Smith as a way of challenging Woolman by revealing his imperfections.

> Last night in my Sleep I thought I was in a Room with thee, and thou drawing thy chair nigh mine, did, in a friendly way, tell me of Sundry particular failings thou had observed in me, and Expressd some desire that I might do better. I felt inwardly thankfull for thy care over me, and made little other reply than to tell thee that I took it very kind.[2]

The following day he writes another letter to John Smith.

> Some pt. of thy first and longest letter has had a particular and frequent place in my Consideration, and I think has done me a little good.[3]

Although the specifics of his brokenness are not revealed, their relationship must have been a deep and loving one in which John Woolman was able to receive unflattering views of himself, views he took seriously and acknowledged and was, through reflection and his intimacy with God, able to see and accept God's invitation to grow. He was able to see the love in the criticism.

He also revealed to John Smith his human doubts about his discerned call and the price he, and Sarah, had to pay for being faithful.

> I am about to leave home under much thoughtfulness, & at times it Seems to border upon distress of Mind.[4]

Due to John Woolman's awareness of his own brokenness, as Reginald Reynolds notes,

> he did not try to stir up feeling against those who had power or possessions, but endeavoured to arouse the feelings of those very people and to quicken their consciences. He did not stand apart and condemn society, but took upon himself the burden of its guilt.[5]

However, in this, as in all things, he was not perfect.

> Our Quarterly Meeting yesterday being chiefly made up of members of your monthly Meeting, I find the Humbling power of Truth Engaging me to Inform you. That in the debate that then was, I am sorrowfully sensible that I did not keep low enough in my mind so as to have my Speech & Conduct thoroughly seasoned with the Meekness of Wisdom — and this I do in regard to His cause who mercifully looked upon me in that distress of mind which I was under soon after the meeting endeth.[6]

He had become clear that he had spoken in an unhelpful way, i.e. had not spoken from the Silence. In fact, *he* had spoken rather than allowing God to speak through him. With a contrite heart, he apologises. John Woolman was a person who, through the practice of attentiveness, was sensitive to his inner movements and was able to discern between the times when he was speaking and the times when God was speaking through him.

As will be seen in other examples, John Woolman desired to uphold the practices of his faith community, their commitment to God, and the true discernment of God's call. As a result of his rigorous honesty, he is willing to embarrass himself before his peers for his embarrassment is less important than being faithful.

What is elicited when someone is willing to share from the depths of their journey to God, when someone is willing to let their wounds be laid open? Others are set free to share of their journey, doubts, fears, and joy. Community grows and deeper sharing ensues, and mutual support for our individual and collective ministries takes on a new, richer form.

The temptations of the earthly life are great. Relying on God is the only way to resist the temptations. Strength is needed for some will be offended by the path we take. But in these times of trial, do we turn to God at first or only as a last resort?

> And now on thy part, after thy Sore Affliction and doubts of recovery, thou art again restored, forget not Him who hath helped thee, but in humble gratitude hold fast his instructions, thereby to shun those by paths which leads from the firm foundation. I am Sensible of that variety of Company, to which one in thy business must be Exposed. I have painfully felt the force of Conversation proceeding from men deeply rooted in an Earthly mind, and can sympathize with others in Such Conflicts, in that much weakness still attends me. .
> . . .
>
> The fear of man brings a snare: by halting in our duty, & giveing back in the time of tryal, our hands grow weaker, our Spirits get mingled with the people, our ears grow dull as to hearing the language of the True Shepherd; that when we look at the way of the

Righteous, it seems as though it was not for us to follow them.

There is a love Cloaths my mind while I write, which is superior to all Expressions, & I find my heart open to encourage to a holy Emulation to advance forward in Christian firmness. Deep Humility is a Strong Bulwark; & as we enter into it, we find safety and true Exaltation.[7]

Veils can fall over our eyes, making it harder to discern God's call. At times, we actively practice not listening to God. Perhaps the way of Truth seems not to be for us; it may seem extreme, inhuman, antisocial, or too much to pay. Our minds become filled with rationalisations why *our* path is the better one, or why *this* is all that we can do. We limit ourselves for we have not really acknowledged the giftedness that God has given us. We place low expectations on ourselves and so cause self-injury. At times, this self-limiting is through doing too much, filling all our space until there is no room for the quiet voice of God to be heard. *We* act rather than allowing God to act through us.

I am humbly Thankfull to My Gracious Father, who has brought my mind in a good degree to be resigned to him.

From Him my being is derived. . . . All I have are his gifts, and I am endeavouring (though in weakness) to Surrender all to him.[8]

And John Woolman knows there is more growth possible when "in a good degree to be resigned to him." This is also a recognition that part of his will has still to be handed over to God to be transformed into God's will. A great challenge. His desire is to surrender, but he is aware of his own brokenness, his own resistance. And he recognises that his ever-deepening surrender to God is a process of his cooperation with the graces God is offering, the graces God is always offering.

Returning from a teaching assignment in another town, I arrived on the outskirts of Shepparton, Victoria, feeling tired and a bit bewildered by all the signs of the consumer society that greeted me. A voice in my head said, Why not give in to it? Why fight it? What is the point? What difference am I making? Where do we draw the line? Are we clear where the line is for us? Are we aware of the temptations? Where is God's call leading us? In which ways is God asking us to stand against worldly values and encompass God's values?

We all make compromises with the worldly values in our society, but do we do it consciously? Where do we need help in dealing with our brokenness? Which temptation is God currently asking us to resist? Do we ask God to help us?

They who dwell on lands as their inheritance, who eat the food which they rais, and wear garments of their own work, and of many others appear to be the least exposed to temptation. Even these stand daily in need of Divine assistance to support their minds in uprightness before the Lord. But when I think on the various kinds of traffick which are in some degree connected with that spirit which works in disobedient children, and on the deficulties and temptations which attends trade in the present condition of countries, I have often felt a particular tenderness toward and care for those who depend on merchandise for a living.[9]

The gap that exists between the life we profess and the way we live is a constant challenge. This gap also existed for John Woolman, and at times he was willing to compromise his principles.

Beloved friend John Townsend

If any letter comes to thy hand directed to me, I desire thou may open it in private, and show it to no one, and if thou believe it [to] be of a nature greatly requiring haste, then send it by the post, else keep it till other opportunity of conveyance.

Thy loving friend, John Woolman[10]

John Woolman recognised God's presence with him in his brokenness and knew of God's suffering with his suffering. And in the midst of this there is hope for God is calling us forth into new life. God does not give up on us. The enlivened faith community, the bride, will be adorned for her husband (Isaiah 62).

> I feel a pure and Holy Spirit in a weak & broken Constitution: this Spirit within me hath suffered deeply and I have born my part in the Suffering, that there may come forth a Church pure & clean like the New Jerusalem, as a Bride Adorned for her husband.[11]

As we grow closer to God, the more deeply do we feel the abomination of our sinfulness for we become ever more conscious of God's unconditional love for us. The pain is even greater when it arises from an abandonment of a previously received grace. But God will not turn us away. God is only waiting for the opportunity to heal us. At times, however, it can be very difficult to uphold that vision of hope in the midst of our sinfulness.

> Under this Anguish of Soul, evident to all about him, he [John Woolman] Stood up on his feet, tho' week, and with a Lamentable Voice Cryed mightily to God that he would have Mercy upon him, a Miserable Siner for that he had Lately, under Extream weakness, given up the purity of his Testimony against the West India trade, In partaking freely of rum and Molasses; After long Conflict with these Horrors, he appeared more Easy, as believing God would be gracious to him. He now informed us he had found the mercys of God to be toward him, and that he had an Evidence of Inward

Peace, and that God had Excepted of his great conflict with the power of darkness the fore part of this Night.[12]

To enter upon the journey into God is no easy task for we have an inbuilt resistance to facing our pain. But it is necessary, manageable, and life-giving. An unwillingness to face our frailty leads to an inner death. Christ taught the people as they were able to bear it. God does not bring up issues we cannot deal with, even if we find them difficult — this is an act of God's perfect discernment and tenderness. God is intimately aware of our state and loves us unconditionally.

In his letter to Elizabeth Smith, John Woolman speaks out of his love for her, their connectedness, and his knowledge of his own incompleteness. This is not a letter that can be written to a stranger. He says there are lessons for her to learn, and he acknowledges that he is still learning too. He affirms that God has been working in her life — and so challenges her to live up to her experience of what is life-giving, to the "purity of her principles." And he ends with a message of prayer and love.

> [The Truth my dear sister, hath been precious in thy sight and I trust remains to be to thee precious as ever.]
> . . . .
> Christ of old time taught the people as they were able to bear it, and I believe, my dear friend, there are lessons for thee and I (sic) yet to learn. Friends from the Country and in the Citty are often at thy house, and when they behold amongst thy furniture some things which are not agreeable to the purity of Truth, the minds of some, I believe, at times are in danger of being diverted from so close an attention to the Light of Life as is necessary for us. . . .
>
> . . . I trust the Great Friend and Keeper is near thee, in Whose Love I am thy friend.[13]

What a wonderful example this is of the Christ in John Woolman speaking to the Christ in another. The above letter is not theoretical for he recognises the temptations from his own experience. Writing to John Wilson, he states,

> When I followed the Trade of a Tailor, I had a feeling of that which pleased the proud mind in people; & growing uneasie, was strengthened to leave off that which was superfluous in my Trade.[14]

And in the same letter, he writes:

> When I was at your house, I believe I had a sense of the pride of people being gratified in some of the business thou followest, and feel a concern in pure love to endeavour to inform thee of it.

> Christ our leader is worthy of being followed in his leadings at all times. The enemy gets many on his side.

> O! that we may not be divided between the two, but may be wholly on the side of Christ.

> In true love to you all I remain thy friend

> > John Woolman[15]

We are held in God's love as we encounter and acknowledge our brokenness and receive God's forgiveness.

> [H]e whose tender mercies are over all his works hath placed a principle in the human mind which incites to exercise goodness toward every living creature; and this being singly attended to, people become tender-hearted and sympathizing, but being frequently and totally rejected, the mind sets itself up in a contrary disposition. . . .

> . . . I felt remorse in my mind, and getting home I retired and prayed to the Lord to forgive me.[16]

And from the freedom of forgiveness our desire to be obedient grows. Our desire to place ourselves in God's hands grows. Our desire to be part of the Kingdom of God grows.

But let us trust in God, who will not suffer us to be tempted above what we are able to bear but will with the temptation also make a way to escape it.[17]

With God's assistance, as we stand against our brokenness, we grow stronger and desire to be filled with the Holy Spirit.

[W]e may see ourselves cripled and halting, and from a strong bias to things pleasant and easie, find an impossibility to advance forward: but things impossible with men are possible with God.[18]

[B]y beholding our own emptiness, we desire to partake of his fullness; by feeling our own poverty, we covet his riches.[19]

In the Strength of all Temptation and in dificulties which Appear very great, there hath seem'd before me a prospect, a POWER, able and ready to subdue all things to Himself.

In a fresh sence of pure Love I remain thy frd.[20]

"In a fresh sense of pure love" – in other words, the Holy Spirit gives clarity and freedom.

I believe my ufferings in this broken Nature are now nearly Accomplished, & my Father hath Shewed me that the Holy Spirit that now works within me, may work in young lively Constitutions & may strengthen them to travel up and down the world in the feeling of pure Wisdom, that many may believe them & the purity of their Lives & learn Instruction.[21]

There will be times when we will be tempted, as Jesus in the desert, to condemn others, to think grandly of ourselves, etc. These times of temptation are unavoidable. But God is always there. Always ready to help,

The steadfast love of the Lord never ceases,
his mercies never come to an end;
they are new every morning.

Lamentations 3:22–23 NRSV

Letters: 1761 to November 1763

1761 to Hannah White

I have often looked at a life conformable to the wisdom and policy of man, where our wills have an open field to move in. And I have looked at a self denying humble life where the creature falling upon the true cornerstone is broken. This latter way of life to me appears most precious; and this day it came upon me to look attentively towards the manners, the spirit, and disposition that appears common amongst the people, and I said in my heart, how few dwell deep enough.

How few amongst the young men live in self denial, and manifest true heavenly mindedness; and I was careful for thee, that thou when looking towards them, might prize that which is most valuable and understand that the nearest approach to pure celestial happiness is the furthest distance from the ways and spirit of this world. I felt a little engagement which arose not from enquiry, nor from hearing, but from unfeigned love.

John Woolman[1]

17 November 1761, to Israel Pemberton

Beloved Friend

The piece J. Churchman took home he perus'd, but being taken poorly, made no remark in writing on it. My brother Asher being at their last Monthly Meeting, and I writing to J. C. about it, he sent it, and George, I expect by his agreement, sent a letter to me refering it to me carefully to review it and transcribe it. Since which I have spent some time therein, and am now come to Town in order that, if way should open for Friends to meet again upon it, I may be near in Case they should want to speak with me. I am a little Cautious of being much at thy House, on acct. of the Small pox, but would gladly meet thee at Such house as thou thinks Sutable, to have a little Conversation with thee.

I have not yet offered it to any of the Committee. I lodge at Reuben Haines', and am mostly there.

I remain thy loveing f'rd

John Woolman.

17: 11 : 1761

Endorsed, "For Israel Pemberton, when he comes home." By I. P.

"From John Woolman, about his treatise."[2]

22 November 1761, to Samuel Smith

Beloved Friend

As the appointmt at our last meeting was Submitted to, if we prepare no Essay, it will require some Apology, and thou, I expect, art likely to be Absent. As Sending a Short Epistle will, I hope, have no ill tendency, I, on thinking further on it, Seem'd inclined to make an Essay which I send herewith.

If thou art Easie that one Should go, and would be pleased to look over and Alter this as it appears best to thee and Send it back, I would Endeavour to Copy as many as there are Mo[nthly] Meetings.

I remain thy loving frd

John Woolman[3]

Late 1761, to Israel Pemberton

Beloved Friend: As I expect to go out of Town (if well) in the Morning, and it's likely, may not Se thee, I thought it best to Acquaint thee That I remain Well satisfied with what thou propos'd relating to the preface, and though I have look'd over the piece with Some care and done according to the best of my Understanding, I have all along been apprehensive that if it be made publick There was a further labour for some other person necessary, and if thou can feel liberty from thy other concerns, and freedom to Spend some time in a deliberate reviewing and correcting of it, and make such alterations or additions as thou believes may be usefull, the prospect of it is agreeable to me.

In true brotherly love I remain thy fr'd

John Woolman.

Same evening, after we met.

The committee gave it to Anthony (Benezet) with a message with it to thee. J. W.[4]

9 February 1762, to Israel Pemberton

Beloved Friend

Since I saw thee I have been thoughtful in case some of the first part should be printed, whether it would not be best to have them, or a part of them, stitched Separate. As they have been pleanty (sic) in and about these parts, I expect some would chuse to have one of the Second part who of Choise would not take both together; that it hath been a query with me if the First part be printed, whether a less Number would not be sufficient of them than the Second.

Having thus hinted what I had thought, I am free to leave it to friends, either to omit printing them, or to print as many as to you may appear best.

With love to thee and family I remain thy loveing fr'd,

John Woolman.[5]

20 April 1762, to Rebecca Jones

Beloved Friend,

As thou offered me a book on the basic terms of calling for it and I when in town did not take it, I think good to acquaint thee, that the offer I consider as a kindness to me, that I have a desire to peruse the book, and that I once came to thy house when last in town to speak with thee about it. Though it so fell out that I saw thee not.

I had an intent and enclination to have spent a little time at thy house but through some other engagements together with the reason above mentioned was prevented.

To Him who is a Father, a counceler and safe protecter to His family, through the various deficulties which attend them in this world, I recomend thee and my beloved friend thy companion,

and remain your friend

John Woolman[6]

20 June 1762, to Israel Pemberton

Beloved Friend:

As true love moves on our Minds we find them turned at times toward certain places & particular persons, and yet unable to give any reason why they are turned that way any more than another – and Such is my case at present.

My Mind of late hath been with thee more than usual, & I seem at liberty to open to thee the manner in which I have looked toward thee.

In those small affairs of life which have fallen to my lot to be concerned in, I have at times found that which has appeared difficult to Manage as a Christian, and

Looking at thy Scituation Amidst many Affairs, & at the family thou hast the care of, I have felt, as I believe, some degree of thy burthen.

I have had in view the purity of the Heavenly Family. The most Gracious and most tender Visitations of Christ to our Souls drawing them from the mixture and entanglements, that they may Attain true Liberty, and have seem'd in company with thee, looking for and desiring a more perfect Deliverance. ~ Satan?

In the Strength of all Temptation and in dificulties which Appear very great, there hath seem'd before me a prospect, a POWER, able and ready to subdue all things to Himself.

In a fresh sence of pure Love I remain thy frd

John Woolman.

I send these by Wm. Calvert with request
to deliver them into thy hand.[7]

4 April 1763, to John Smith

Beloved Friend

The Corps of an honest Friend being to be buried at our Meeting House today, an inclination to attend the Burial occasions my Absence from Meeting.

I find nothing to hinder a Certificate from being prepared for our Friend, John Sleeper.

4: 4: 1763   I remain thy loving friend,

John Woolman.

Friends concern'd in the Affair of E. Large's Estate need be under no difficulty in regard to appointing a time on my account. I am at present under no particular appointment on any business that I remember. J. W.[8]

4 June 1763, to his brother Uriah Woolman

From what past in conversation I was in hopes of thy company a few days at my house. But as an opertunity of that kind hath been wanting I take this way to inform thee before I go of that which I have felt on thy account.

A belief in the allsufficiency of God, and in His care in providing for those that fear Him hath often afforded comfort to me, not only in regard to my self, but allso with relation to my fellow creatures whom I love, and who have the same need of His Fatherly help as I have.

They who dwell on lands as their inheritance, who eat the food which they raise, and wear garments of their own work, and of many others appear to be the least exposed to temptation. Even these stand daily in need of Divine assistance to support their minds in uprightness before the Lord. But when I think on the various kinds of traffick which are in some degree connected with that spirit which works in disobedient children, and on the deficulties and temptations which attends trade in the present condition of countries, I have often felt a particular tenderness toward and care for those who depend on merchandise for a living. And when my mind hath been thus filled with care and affection, mixed with a feeling of the manifold deficulties attending business, a fresh sense of God's goodness in guiding his people [undecipherable] qualifying with sound judgement to distinguish things that differ, and in preserving them from inward dangers, hath felt very precious to me. And thou hath often on this account been the object of my hearty desires.

As I was lately transcribing some notes I made in the southern parts when thee and I were there together, my mind was brought to feel over again some heavy labours which I believe we had both some share of, and to desire we might ever attend to Him whose fatherly regard was extended toward us in that lonely journey –

I remain thy loving brother John Woolman[9]

8 June 1763, to Sarah Woolman

about sunset

I am now at Bethlehem, a Moravian town, and midling well in company with John Pemberton, Wm. Lightfoot & Benjamin Parvin. . . . William and Benjamin Expect to go forward to fort Allen on the Frontier. Then William Expects to turn home. And as to Benjamin – His mind at present seems so Engaged that he Shews no Inclination to leave me: I have had Some weighty Conversation with Him and let him know that I am quite free to go alone if his way does not appear clear to Him. My Indian Companions appear friendly & shew I think quite as much regard for me as they did at our first meeting at Philad[elphi)a.

There is nothing to me appears aniways discouraging more than what Thou knew of when I was with thee. I am humbly Thankfull to the Lord that my mind is so supported in a Trust in Him that I go cheerfully on my Journey and at present Apprehend that I have nothing in any way to fear but a Spirit of Disobedience, which I Trust through Divine Help I may be delivered from.

That Pure Light which Enlightens every man coming into the World to me appears as Lovely as Ever. To the guidance of which I hope thee and I may Attend while we live in this world, and then all will be well.

With Endeared love to thee and my Daughter & my Dear friends and Neighbours I conclude thy most Affectionate

Husband John Woolman

(Note in margin) My Companions Express a Sympathizing love to thee.[10]

16 June 1763, to Israel Pemberton and Sarah Woolman

Dear Fr'd

We are now well near Wahalowsing in Company with Job Chilaway & several Indians from Wahalowsing and Some from Else where who appear Civil & kind. ☺

John Woolman.

the Company of B. Parvin is Comfortable to me.

My dear and tender wife

A Sence of Alsufficiency of God in Supporting those who trust in Him in all the Dispensations of His Providence wherein they may be tryed feels comfortable to me in my Journey.

My Daily Labour is to find a full Resignedness to Him and m(a)y say with thankfullness He Remains to be my Gracious Father.

To Him I recommend thee, my Dear Companion, greatly Desiring thy mind may be Resigned to Him for I Veryly believe if we keep in this Frame all will End well.

I write in Haste but Remember my Dear Daughter & fr'ds.

John Woolman.

(In margin: "Please send this to Wife.")
        For
Israel Pemberton
        in philada.
to the Care of the
Storekeeper at Shamokin.
pr. Job Chilaway.[11]

27 June 1763, to Israel Pemberton

Burlington, 27da 6mo 1763 1 o'clock.

Dear Friend,

Through the mercies of the Lord my Belovd Companion and helpmate B. Parvin and I were helped to perform our Journey to Wahalousing and came back to Bethlehem on Seventh day night was yesterday at the Swamp Meeting and I lodged last night at John Cadwaleders and am now hasting home – Our Journey though attended with much deep Exercise hath been greatly to our Satisfaction. We were at seven Religious meetings with the Indians many of which people I believe were in these troublous times greatly Comforted in our visit and they all appeared kind & loving to us — I saw nothing amongst any of them in that place which to me appeard like disaffection to the English — but our Conversation was mostly with the soberer sort. The Moravian Preacher who was there when I went and continued there while I stayd appeard kind and courteous from first to last and I believe his intentions are honest.

In a humbling sense of His goodness in whom my poor Soul has trusted, I remain with kind Love to thee and family and all my Dear frd

John Woolman

[I have the horse with me in pretty good order, and I expect to keep him well a while and send him.][12]

29 November 1763, to Chesterfield Monthly Meeting

To the Monthly Meeting to be held at Chesterfield 1:12: 1763

Our Quarterly Meeting yesterday being chiefly made up of members of your monthly Meeting, I find the Humbling power of Truth Engaging me to Inform you. That in the debate that then was, I am sorrowfully sensible that I did not keep low enough in my mind so as to have my Speech & Conduct thoroughly seasoned with the Meekness of Wisdom — and this I do in regard to His cause who mercifully looked upon me in that distress of mind which I was under soon after the meeting endeth.

John Woolman[13]

30 November 1763, to Israel Pemberton

Beloved Friend,

On enquiring I could find no house suitable, either at Mount Holly or Rancocus. I then thought of staying [with] friends at the end of a week day meeting to open the case to Y.M. But the two next meetings were small, partly by weather, and I then concluded to wait till this day which hath been our preparatory meeting, and in the meantime spoke to several about it.

I opened it today before friends parted, and they thought best to defer the consideration of building a house. And in the meantime have agreed with a man to get a quantity of wood suitable for baskets, and send by a flat as a present to Y.M.

I expect Wm. Calvert will bring this to town by whom we expect to hear more about Y.M.

With love to thee and thy family, I remain your friend

John Woolman[14]

Holy Obedience: Abandonment to God

One thing is clear, that there is a will and intention of God bearing upon me, and I must let it bear fully upon me, so that I may be free. My life has no meaning except as a conscious and total self dedication to the *fulfillment of His intentions*, which, in their details, remain a complete mystery.

Amen!

Thomas Merton, *A Vow of Conversation*[1]

Here we have a prospect of one common interest from which our own is inseparable — that to turn all the treasures we possess into the channel of universal love becomes the business of our lives.

John Woolman, "A Plea for the Poor"[2]

The mystical experience contains an invitation to action. From the place of deep prayer arises our call to be ministers. In the Silence we are given much, and much will be asked of us. To minister requires the gifts of humility and perseverance and the recognition that though we may be invited to do what we find difficult, it is not difficult for God.

[A]s offending sober people is disagreeable to my inclination, I was straitened in my mind; but as I looked to the Lord, he inclined my heart to his testimony. . . .
. . . I had a fresh confirmation that acting contrary to present outward interest from a motive of divine love and in regard to truth and righteousness, and thereby incurring the resentments of people, opens the way to a treasure better than silver and to a friendship exceeding the friendship of men.[3]

But the fear of the Lord so covered me at times that way was made easier than I expected.[4]

Kathryn Damiano, whom I met at Pendle Hill in 1994, wrote to me:

> God is with us and Christ's guidance is available at all times, even for the smallest things. Christ is alive now. Christ is not dead. That is where early Friends got their life. They felt the power of God when they worshipped together and in their individual lives.[5]

In the midst of our struggles, we are sometimes tempted to give up. We lose sight of God's power flowing through us. The way of the world is sometimes attractive for it appears easy. But this is so only superficially for it is in reality deathly rather than life-giving.

However, if we are willing to trust in God, if we will allow God to help us, all is possible. We can stand against all temptations if we are tempered by the purifying, healing fire of God's love. The choice is ours. God is always knocking.

John Woolman was called, and he acted on the call.

> I feel my mind resigned to leave you for a season, to exercise that gift which the Lord hath bestowed on me, which though small compared with some, yet in this I rejoyce, that I feel love unfeigned toward my fellow-creatures.[6]

> Our wills being made Subject to his, all temptations are Surmountable.[7]

God does not lay the notion of perfection upon us. This is a human invention that is a burden God does not ask us to carry. God accepts and loves us in our imperfect state. But we are invited to seek clarity, and we are encouraged by God's love to be faithful to the call we receive.

Margaret O'Neal, a fellow resident student at Pendle Hill in the spring of 1994, wrote to me:

> My soul has been heavy all day — because this morning I didn't listen to a nudging from God. Sometimes I have a hard time being sure of God's voice. Especially when it is something I don't want to hear! How difficult it is to walk this path we're walking. . . . And blessed . . .

> It is by listening to God in these small nudgings that I bind myself to God.

> I've realised that when I speak of "listening" to God, I equate listening with obeying. It doesn't seem like listening to God if I respond with: "Well, thanks for your input, but I've decided to do otherwise." The only reasonable response to the voice of God is to obey. What a miracle it is to *hear* God's voice; how could I possibly choose to defy it?

> But I did this morning. I just wasn't *sure* of what I heard. . . . May my soul be enlightened so that I may recognise the presence of God.[8]

Thomas Merton states:

> My Lord God, I have no idea where I am going. I do not see the road ahead of me. I cannot know for certain where it will end. Nor do I really know myself, and the fact that I think I am following your will does not mean I am actually doing so. But I believe that the desire to please you does in fact please you. And I hope I have that desire in all that I am doing. I hope that I will never do anything apart from that desire. And I know that if I do this you will lead me by the right road, though I may know nothing of that. Therefore I will trust you always though I may seem to be lost and in the shadow of death. I will not fear,

for you are ever with me, and you will never leave me to face my perils alone.[9]

John Woolman wrote:

I may say with thankfulness that the kindness of Providence is still near to his people, to give counsel in times of distress and difficulty. The need we have of His help some of late have been more sensible than heretofore.[10]

John Woolman's commitment to be obedient to God arises from his experiential knowledge of God's Love for him and all creation. His desire to abandon himself to God is a natural movement of the Spirit in a person who has been willing to receive God's love.

My heart hath been often melted into contrition since I left thee, under a Sence of divine goodness being extended for my help and preparing in me a Subjection to his will.[11]

Accepting Christ's presence, Christ's tenderness, Christ's desires for us, leads us on the path of freedom. We become detached from worldly values and journey toward true liberty.

John Woolman saw himself as walking in the company of his friend Israel Pemberton and in the company of Christ. They allowed themselves to be led from their entanglements into a state of nakedness and freedom, their souls looking for and desiring a more perfect deliverance.

I have had in view the purity of the Heavenly Family. The most Gracious and most tender Visitations of Christ to our Souls drawing them from the mixture and entanglements, that they may Attain true Liberty, and have seem'd in company with thee, looking for and desiring a more perfect Deliverance.[12]

The power of Good is greater than the power of evil. In all our difficulties, Christ is present and is a power for good. Do we believe that?

When we are well, do we remember the God who was with us in our sickness and helped us to recover? Do we believe that God was/is with us in our sickness? Do we turn to God at first or only as a last resort? What sort of relationship do we have with God? What is our image of God?

Let us rejoice in God's goodness to us and undertake to follow in God's way. May God help us to resist the temptation to step off the foundations God has laid for us.

But we must acknowledge the difficulty of this calling, for in truth it is difficult. We, by the nature of society, are forever interacting with those who are not following God's way, good people trapped within institutions and structures which are death-giving, including religious bodies. We should always remember that we have much to learn from the holy people who have never set foot in church and do not use the word God.

We are invited to desire the strength to stand in the Light of Truth.

> But in humble gratitude hold fast his instructions, thereby to shun those by paths which leads from the firm foundation. I am Sensible of that variety of Company, to which one in thy business must be Exposed. I have painfully felt the force of conversation proceeding from men deeply rooted in an Earthly mind, and can sympathize with others in Such Conflicts, in that much weakness still attends me.[13]

> In the Strength of all Temptation and in dificulties which Appear very great, there hath seem'd before me a

prospect, a POWER, able and ready to subdue all things to Himself.[14]

When we are called to minister, God is asking us to be helpful, in some way, to others. But we are asked to do this humbly for the power comes from God working through us. John Woolman recognised that God knew what was best for those he visited; i.e. God was there before John Woolman turned up and would be present after he had gone. And, he recognised that he, John Woolman, would not necessarily see the fruits of his labour.

Ministering is reminiscent of planting seeds and not knowing what will come. Will we be surprised by small white daffodils amidst the irises?

Do we ever really know what is happening in the depths of another human being?

Indeed, it is desirable only to get occasional hints of the fruits. This leads to prayers of thanksgiving, gives enough encouragement to continue, elicits a state of detachment from the outcome, and leads to a state of inner freedom, a place from which true ministry can take place.

We are also called to minister because *we* need our ministry to get closer to God.

> Our Visits in general have hitherto been in weakness, and to me it hath been a time of Abasement. I hope, notwithstanding, our appointing meetings have not been to the dishonour of Truth. My Exercises have, I think, been at least usefull to me, & I am thankfull to the Almighty in that I have seen and felt that He knows best what is for our good, and the good of fr'ds where we come.[15]

As he ministers, John Woolman detects the invitation to abandon himself even more to God. His desire is to surrender totally to God. How important it is to recognise and state our desires, for God will not force us. Stating our desires points us in a direction, and we grow even closer to God. It confirms our dependence on God and leads us to clarity and real freedom.

John Woolman is in a state of continually reflecting on his experience and is always learning of God. As he travels in the ministry, he is on a journey *with* God. He knew his travelling in the ministry was the right thing to do when he left home, and he is still very clear.

> But Such is the weight of the work I am engaged in, and Such the baptisms with which I have been baptized; that I see A Necessity for all nature to Stand Silent. . . .
>
> . . . All I have are his gifts, and I am endeavouring (though in weakness) to Surrender all to him.[16]
>
> Every Year brings Additional Experience and I think I never more clearly Saw the reasonableness and fitness of Casting all my cares on God than I have Since I left thee.[17]

With his desire to be obedient to God's call and his need to be supported by God, his task each day is to give himself over to God. God is faithful to John Woolman, and John Woolman is faithful to God.

> I am humbly Thankfull to the Lord that my mind is so supported in a Trust in Him that I go cheerfully on my Journey and at present Apprehend that I have nothing in any way to fear but a Spirit of Disobedience, which I Trust through Divine Help I may be delivered from.[18]
>
> My Daily Labour is to find a full Resignedness to Him and m(a)y say with thankfullness he Remains to be my Gracious Father.[19]

In describing Holy Obedience in *A Testament of Devotion*, Thomas Kelly writes:

> Only now and then comes a man or a woman who, like John Woolman or Francis of Assisi, is willing to be utterly obedient, to go the other half, to follow God's faintest whisper. But when such a commitment comes in a human life, God breaks through, miracles are wrought, world-renewing divine forces are released, history changes.[20]

People like John Woolman are presented to us as arrows pointing to the universal invitation. If, in the midst of admiring him, we leave it at that, we are missing the point. His witness is there to challenge us to follow God across our human-made boundaries.

John Woolman encouraged others to be obedient to God, and he lived a life that inspired others to live in a way closer to God's values. His recognition of the holiness of God and his knowledge of the blessed state that could exist if we gave ourselves over to the Divine Teacher meant he became distressed when others, particularly children, were educated into materialistic ways — by the education system and through the example of others.

> My mind is often on the immutability of the Divine being, & the purity of his judgments, and a prospect of outward distress in this part of the world hath been open before me, and I have had to behold the blessedness of a state in which the mind is fully subjected to the divine Teacher, and the confusion and perplexity of such who profess the Truth, and are not faithful to the leadings of it: nor have I ever felt pitty move more evidently on my mind, than I have felt it toward children, who, by their education, are lead on in unnecessary expenses, and exampled in seeking gain in the wisdom of this world to support themselves

therein.[21]

In this thy late affliction I've found a deep fellow-feeling with thee, and had a secret hope throughout that it might please the Father of Mercies to raise thee up & sanctifie thy troubles to thee, that thou being more fully acquainted with that way which the world esteems foolish may feel the Cloathing of Divine Fortitude, and be strengthened to Resist that spirit which leads from the Simplicity of the Everlasting Truth.[22]

To Him I recomend thee, my Dear Companion, greatly Desiring thy mind may be Resigned to Him for I Veryly believe if we keep in this Frame all will End well.[23]

On 9 July 1769, John Woolman wrote a letter to a now unknown recipient. The thrust of this letter is to comment on the pressure of worldly values on religious considerations, e.g. time and money. He is writing a supportive letter to this friend whom he feels, like himself, is being asked to be an example of the True Way.

My dear friend — In our meeting of Ministers and Elders, I have several times felt the movings of divine love amongst us, and to me there appeared a preparation for profitable labours in the meeting: but the time appointed for publick meetings drawing near, a strictness for time hath been felt. And in Yearly Meeting, for the preservation of good order in the Society, when much business hath lain before us, and weighty matters relating to the Testimony of Truth hath been under consideration, I have sometimes felt that a care in some to get forward soon hath prevented so weighty and deliberate a proceeding as by Some hath been desired.

Sincere hearted friends who are concerned to wait for the Counsel of Truth, are often made helps to each other, and when such from distant parts of our extensive Yearly meeting, have set their houses in order and thus gathered in one place, I believe it is the will of our Heavenly Father, that we, with a single eye to the leadings of his Holy Spirit, should quietly wait on him without hurrying in the business before us.

As my mind hath been on these things some difficulties have arisen in my way; first there are through prevailing custom, many expences attending our entertainment in town, which, if the readings of Truth were faithfully followed, might be lessened.

Many under an outward shew of a delicate life, are entangled in the worldly Spirit, labouring to support those expensive customs which they at times feel to be a burden.

These expences arising from a conformity to the spirit of this world, have often lain as a heavy burden on my mind, and Especially at the time of our solemn meetings; and a life truly conformable to the simplicity that is in Christ, where we may faithfully serve our God without distraction, and have no interruption from that which is against the Truth, to me hath been very desirable; and my dear friend, as the Lord in Infinite mercies hath called thee and I (Sic) to labour at times in his vineyard, and hath, I believe, sometimes appointed to us different offices in his work, our opening our experience one to another in the pure feeling of Charity may be profitable.

The great Shepherd of the Sheep I believe is preparing some to example the people in a plain Simple way of living. And I feel a tender care that thee and I may abide in that, where our light may shine clear, and nothing pertaining to us have any tendency to Strengthen those customs which are distinguishable from the Truth as it is in Jesus.

The great Shepherd of the Sheep I believe is preparing some to example the people in a plain Simple way of living. And I feel a tender care that thee and I may abide in that, where our light may shine clear, and nothing pertaining to us have any tendency to Strengthen those customs which are distinguishable from the Truth as it is in Jesus.[24]

God loves us even more than our parents love us, more than any human being can. God desires that we become whole and be in union with God. What is our desire? Are we willing to pay the price? Are we ready for the discipline and obedience that are necessary?

God is waiting for us to invite Her into our hearts to heal our inner conflicts, to heal our inner distress, to heal our negative view of ourselves, to expand our limited view of God, to expand our limited view of our potential. Our pain contains an invitation from God to address our inner state. But we must be willing to pass through the pain of the struggle. We must be willing to believe that God shows us our difficulties when we are ready to deal with them.

If kind parents love their children and delight in their happiness, then He who is perfect goodness in sending abroad mortal Contagions, doth Assuredly direct their use. Are the righteous removed by it? their change is hapy: Are the wicked taken away in their wickedness? the Almighty is clear. Do we pass through it with anguish and great bitterness, & yet recover? he intends that we should be purged from dross, and our ear opened to discipline.[25]

If we will allow God to set us free, we will enter into a state of reliance upon and obedience to God — a place where we will trust that we will be given all that we need, a place of spiritual, psychological, and emotional well-being. As St. Ignatius of Loyola wrote in his classic Suscipe prayer:

Take, Lord, and receive all my liberty,
my memory, my understanding,

and my entire will.
All I have and call my own.

You have given all to me.
To you, Lord, I return it.

Everything is yours; do with it what you will.
Give me only your love and your grace,
that is enough for me.[26]

Letters: April 1769 to January 1771

4 April 1769, to Israel Pemberton

Beloved Friend

As I spoke to thee concerning sending intelligence of vessels sailing I seem free to inform thee that I fe[e]l easie at this time without hearing on that subject and I am desirous to give thee no unnecessary care.

Amidst some dificulties I am comforted in this that I feel love to the brethre[n] and amongst others towards thee.

John Woolman[1]

10 May 1769, to J. C.

Beloved Fr'd

I recd thy letter about a week ago, and having thought some about those herbs mentioned therein I know nothing better at present for me than to write a letter to inform thee, if thou gets it, that if thou art free to get those herbs and prepare electuary, or otherwise to procure it as thou may feel most freedom, I think at present that when it comes to hand, if it comes, I may be free to take some, and to account to thee for it.

I believe the present dispensation is profitable to me and I am often in care that I may be preserved in resignedness and feel for duty from one day to another.

In a degree I hurt of true love.

I remain to thee and thy wife and George

your frd   John Woolman[2]

9 July 1768, to an unknown recipient

Beloved friend:

Since our last Conversation I have felt an increase of brotherly love, and there in a liberty to hint further to thee how at different times for years past, things have wrought on my mind respecting high living.

In some affecting seasons abroad, as I have sat in meetings with desires to attend singly on the pure gift, I have felt that amongst my brethren, grievously entangled in expensive customs, the Lord hath a work for some to do in exampling others in the Simplicity as it is in Christ. II Corinth. XI. 3. As I have seen that a view to live high hath been a stumbling block, and that what some appeared to aim at was no higher than many of the foremost rank in our Society lived, there hath been a labour upon me, that in this respect, the way may be cast up, and the stumbling block taken out of the way of the people. Isaa. 57.14. And here the inexpressible love of Christ in denying himself & enduring grief for our Sakes is often before me, as an example for us to follow, in denying ourselves, of things pleasant to our natural inclinations, that we may example others, in the pure Christian life in our age.

2. In regard to thieves, I have had many Serious thoughts, and often been jealous over myself, lest by withholding from a poor man what our Heavenly Father may intend for him through me, I should lay a temptation in his way to steal, and have often felt a care that no desire for riches, or outward greatness, may prompt me to get that in our house which may create envy, and increase this difficulty.

3. I have sometimes wrote wills for people when sick and expected soon to leave their families who had but little to divide amongst their children, and I have so far

felt a brotherly Sympathy, that their cases have become mine, in regard to a comfortable living for them and here expensive customs have often made the prospect less clear. Expensive customs on such occasions have often Affected me with sadness.

4. The manner of taking possession of the Silver mines Southwestward, the conduct of the conquerors toward the natives, & the miserable toyl of many of our fellow creatures in those mines, have often been the subject of my thoughts; and though I sometimes handle silver and gold as a currency, my so doing is at times attended with pensiveness, and a care that my ears may not be stopped against further instruction; I often think of the fruitfulness of the Soyl where we live, the care that hath been taken to agree with the former owners, the natives, and the conveniences this land affords for our use: and on the numerous oppressions there are in many places, and feel care that my cravings may be rightly bounded, and that no wandering desires may lead me to so Strengthen the hands of the wicked as to partake of their Sins. I. Timo. 5c. 22V.

5. In conversing at times with some well-disposed friends who have been long pressed with poverty, I have thought that some outward help, more than I believed myself a Steward to communicate, might be a blessing to them; and at such times the expenses, that might be saved amongst some of my brethren, without any real inconvenience to them, hath often been brought to my mind; nor have I believed myself clear with out speaking at times publickly concerning it.

6. My mind is often on the immutability of the Divine being, & the purity of his judgments, and a prospect of outward distress in this part of the world hath been open before me, and I have had to behold the blessedness of a state in which the mind is fully subjected to the divine Teacher, and the confusion and

perplexity of such who profess the Truth, and are not faithful to the leadings of it: nor have I ever felt pitty move more evidently on my mind, than I have felt it toward children, who, by their education, are lead on in unnecessary expenses, and exampled in seeking gain in the wisdom of this world to support themselves therein.[3]

16 October 1769, to Israel Pemberton

Belovd Friend

My exercise in regard to being resign'd to go on a visit to some part of the West Indies continue. I expect this week to get (if all is well) three Barrels of Bread baked in our Town, and have thought of sending it first opportunity to thy care if thou art free to take the trouble of storing it. I thought best to get it done at home, that I may see to the doing it in a way to my mind.

I remain thy loving fr'd

John Woolman

I know nothing against going out pretty soon, if way open.[4]

22 October 1769, to unknown recipient

Beloved Friend, I now rec'd thine, and in answer may say if thou knowest of a Vessel anytime soon intended for Barbados and from some knowledge of the circumstances may think it likely to be somewhat agreeable for me, it would be acceptable to be informed of it.

I remain thy loving friend

John Woolman[5]

11 November 1769, to John Pemberton

Belov'd Frd.

I rec'd last Evening a letter from my brother Uriah wrote at the request of James Pemberton informing me that James hath a vessel in port which he expects may Sail for Barbadoes the latter End of this month or beginning of next.

I know not but that I may look toward this Vessel for a passage, but am desirous to inform thee of this my information, as thou Exprest a brotherly care for me respecting a passage.

I remain thy

Loving frd, John Woolman.[6]

17 November 1769, to Israel Pemberton

I yesterday saw a Mattress, and have this Morning agreed for some coarse wool, and expect to make one at home. I feel gratefulness toward thee for thy kind offer, but believe to make one may be best for me.

thy loving frd,
John Woolman.[7]

7 and 13 January 1770 (written by various writers including Woolman; writers recording Woolman's words when he was ill)

This Spirit within me hath suffered deeply and I have born my part in the suffering, that there may come forth a Church pure & Clean like the New Jerusalem, as a bride adorned for her husband. I believe my Sufferings in this broken nature are now nearly Accomplished, & my Father hath Shewed me that the Holy Spirit that now works within me, may work in young lively Constitutions & may strengthen them to travel up & down the world in the feeling of pure Wisdom, that many may believe them & the purity of their Lives & learn Instruction –

Taken from the mouth of my Father as he uttered it in my hearing on a first day meeting while (illegible) . . . ing.[8]

John Woolman himself added the following.

7: 1: 1770, I believe it will be felt by feeling living Members, that that which hath been uttered by my lips has proceeded from the Spirit of Truth, Operating on Mine Understanding, & I meddle not with the Fever.[9]

But the disease progressed, and another watcher recorded:

On 7th day morning about ye 3rd hour, ye 13th of ye 1st Mo. 1770, John Woolman having for Some time lain like a man a Dying, did then call for Water to Wet his tongue for it was Dry, and he wanted to Use it, and then told us then present, that the forepart of the Same night he had very Great horrours on his mind for Departing from the purity of his Testimony, in relation to the West India trafick.

Under this Anguish of Soul, evident to all about him, he Stood up on his feet, tho' week, and with a Lamentable Voice Cryed mightily to God that He would have Mercy upon him, a miserable siner for that he had Lately, under Extream weakness, given up the purity of his Testimony against the West India trade, In partaking freely of rum and Molasses; After long Conflict with these Horrors, he appeared more Easy, as believing God would be gracious to him. He now informed us he had found the mercys of God to be toward him, and that he had an Evidence of Inward Peace, and that God had Excepted of his great conflict with the power of darkness the fore part of this Night.

Uttered by John Woolman's lips and wrote by Aaron Smith.[10]

Prior to 1771, to friends of the Quarterly and Monthly Meetings

Belovd friends –

As I have under an apprehension of duty wrote *Consideration on the true harmony of mankind and how it is to be maintained*, the piece has been inspected by the Overseers of the press and by them agreed to be printed, and the books may be had at the house of ——— for —— ——— per dozen, that being no more than the expense of publishing and covering them.[11]

7 January 1771, to Israel Pemberton

Belovd frd, on reading & considerg thy letter, it appears agreeable that the piece be read in Meeting for Sufferings first. I believe I may be most easie in notice being sent to each of our quarterly Meetings with a number of short Advertis, equal to the number of monthly meetings, that one may be sent to each monthly meeting; and I am free to sign such an Advertisement, first writing them myself, or that my name be put to it, I first seeing a copy if printed, when the books are printed and after a proper time for friends to have notice and to have oportunities of sending for the books, Then what remains (I first taking 300 sheets) may it's likely with less expense be taken of as thou proposd.

With kind Love to thee and thy wife, I remain

your frd
John Woolman
Second day morning[12]

Late 1771, John Woolman's account of Peter Harvey after Harvey's death

In the time of his health, a few months before he departed, I had some loving conversation with him in regard to sundry things in his possession related to his living, which appear'd to be conformable to the Spirit of this world.

He appeared to take my visit very kind, and though he was not fully setled in his mind as to what he should do with them, yet he told me that he was inwardly united to a plain way of living, and to such who in faithfulness walked therein. I was twice with him in his last Sickness, and the first of these times he told me that in his youthful years, his mind was much on improvement in outward business, and that being Successful, many spoke in praise of his conduct, and in this prosperity he got Sundry sorts of Superfluities in workmanship about him and though he had not seen clearly what to do with them; yet he saw that at the time of getting these things he went on in the dark, and they were latterly a burden to his mind.

John Woolman[13]

Under a Sense of His Heavenly Love

Discerning God's call relies on us knowing ourselves and the various ways in which God speaks to us: directly, through another, through the collective wisdom of our faith community, through creation, etc. For John Woolman, discernment was a way of life. It embraced his daily listening to the Spirit, the sharing of his vision with others and encouraging them to reveal their wisdom, and his faithfulness and obedience to his faith community's wisdom. From the depths of his own journey, he also discerned the gifts and burdens of others and gained much knowledge of the spiritual path.

The movements of the Spirit are mysterious and, if we are attentive, will teach us to listen to the nature of God's language to us. For some, words may be seen or heard; perhaps we dream or have visions. Are we affected in the pit of our stomach, the palms of our hands, the soles of our feet, or another place? God speaks to each of us in ways we can understand, even if we cannot understand the reason for the call.

> As true Love moves on our Minds we find them turned at times toward certain places & particular persons, and yet unable to give any reason why they are turned that way any more than another – and Such is my case at present.[1]

> My Exercises have, I think, been at least usefull to me, & I am thankfull to the Almighty in that I have seen and felt that He knows best what is for our good, and the good of fr'ds where we come.[2]

Some of the phrases that John Woolman used to describe his own recognition of God's call are

> ay Father hath shewed
> an evidence of inward peace
> brought my mind in a good degree to be resigned to him
> under a sence of his Heavenly love
> I have seen and felt
> I perceive
> I am free
> true love moves
> fresh sence
> attended with pensiveness
> a care that my ears may not be stopped against
> my mind was opened
> growing uneasie

Beloved Friend

When I followed the Trade of a Tailor, I had a feeling of that which pleased the proud mind in people; & growing uneasie, was strengthened to leave off that which was superfluous in my Trade.[3]

The Truth my dear sister, hath been precious in thy sight and I trust remains to be to thee precious as ever.[4]

The more we practice listening to God (as opposed to practicing not listening to God), the more deeply aware we become of God's call, its subtlety and its quietness. And the more we listen, the less loudly God has to speak, to the point that we know God's presence even if we are suffering.

I believe my Sufferings in this broken Nature are now nearly Accomplished, & my Father hath Shewed me that the Holy Spirit that now works within me, may work in young lively Constitutions & may strengthen them to travel up and down the world in the feeling of pure

Wisdom, that many may believe them & the purity of their Lives & learn Instruction.[5]

The following was written by a person at John Woolman's bedside when he was very ill.

> After long Conflict with these Horrors, he appeared more Easy, as believing God would be gracious to him. He now informed us he had found the mercys of God to be toward him, and that he had an Evidence of Inward Peace, and that God had Excepted of his great conflict with the power of darkness the fore part of this Night.[6]

The Spirit attracts our attention in many ways. Thomas Merton talked of being prompted when working on an old manuscript in his monastery's vault. It may happen when ministering to another or, in the following example from John Woolman, when we are walking and surrounded by nature. But the message only becomes clear when we recognise the prompting and stop to listen.

> Yesterday, as I was walking over a plain on my way to this place, I felt a degree of Divine love attend my mind, and therein an openness toward the children of Stephen Comfort, of which I believed I should endeavour to inform them. My mind was opened to behold the happiness, the safety and beauty of a life devoted to follow the heavenly Shepherd; and a care that the enticements of vain young people may not ensnare any of you.[7]

Discernment is a way of life, not just a process to be pulled off the shelf when a decision is needed. By making discernment a way of being, we build rich foundations from which difficult discernments may be made. Discernment requires a desire to wait, not to push. Although we need to engage in active waiting, which may involve knocking on closed doors, we must always be in a state of patiently waiting to see if God will open that particular door. And if we are unclear, the invitation is to wait.

> I cannot form a concern, but when a concern cometh, I endeavour to be obedient.[8]

> My leaving you under the trying Circumstances now attending you, is not without close exercise and I feel a living concern, that under these cares of business, and under bodily affliction, your minds may be brought to a humble waiting on Him who is the great Preserver of his people.[9]

> The Matter thou mentioned in thy Letter a few days past I had thought a good deal of and talked with Mary about it, but had not seen a clear way to do anything in it.[10]

> Belovd Friend

> My exercise in regard to being resign'd to go on a visit to some part of the West Indies continue [*sic*]. . . . I know nothing against going out pretty soon, if way open.[11]

Travelling in faithfulness, being obedient to our discernment of God's will, we are not often shown a great way ahead. God does not distract us with too large a vision of the future. God knows our weakness to day-dream, to envisage palaces of self-aggrandisement, and, at times, our lack of faith in God's large plan. When Christ said, *Very truly, I tell you, the one who believes in me will also do the works that I do and, in fact, will do greater works than these* (John 14:12 NRSV), do we believe? And so God gives us one small grain of sand at a time. Looking back, we see a beach and are amazed. We are invited, day by day, to discern daily, to be mindful of where we are, and to leave the future to God.

> My journeying hath been through much inward watchfulness. I cannot see far before me. But the Lord, in tender mercy, hath been gracious to me, and way opens for my visit among Friends.[12]

When we express our desires to Christ, we must be careful for we may get what we ask for. Our expressed desires must come from the Heart, that place where God's power resides. In our desire to discern, we are at times given the knowledge of our own pain or others' pain. We will be invited to address issues we may find difficult or easy and joyful. Both will come, and we cannot ask for just the pleasant ones. John Woolman had the strength of faith to be with others in their pain, and he was willing to pay the price of obedience, however great. This takes effort, including a commitment to prayer.

> We have been fellow feelers with the afflicted nor is any affliction too great to endure for the Truth. This I own, and am labouring daily to be found in that resignation.[13]

His daily commitment to a state of resignedness to the will of God reveals God's presence in all things, small and large. He knows too that the act of discerning is not infallible and tests his state of awareness as he travels. Will it be possible to sail to Nantucket? Is this really God's will?

> I wrote from Newport about a week past and Expecting tomorrow if the wind be fair and way open to Sail for Nantucket.[14]

> My mind hath been in an inward watchfull frame Since I left thee, greatly desiring that our proceedings may be Singly in the will of Our Heavenly Father.[15]

> And though I sometimes handle silver and gold as a currency, my so doing is at times attended with pensiveness, and a care that my ears may not be stopped against further instruction.[16]

His awareness of his inner state was not just a navel-gazing exercise but an act of inner obedience that led to outward acts of obedience. His obedience led him to travel in the ministry and to speak to others encouragingly and at times challengingly.

> Haveing been at Sunday Meetings with thee I perceive that He who waits to be gracious to us has given thee among others a distinct sight of the state of the Churches.[17]

> I believed thou understood his language, and I trust thy ear will be attentive to Him, and in that there is safety in the greatest difficulties.[18]

> Beloved friend: Since our last Conversation I have felt an increase of brotherly love, and there in a liberty to hint further to thee how at different times for years past, things have wrought on my mind respecting high living.[19]

Part of the discernment process is to be on the lookout for the tail of the serpent leading us in to actions aligned with worldly values, away from God's will. What is helpful to the people of God? What is harmful? John Woolman was greatly concerned for the life of others and encouraged others to hold fast to the True path. This was a path he trod experientially, not intellectually.

> In some affecting seasons abroad, as I have sat in meetings with desires to attend singly on the pure gift, I have felt that amongst my brethren, grievously entangled in expensive customs, the Lord hath a work for some to do in exampling others in the Simplicity as it is in Christ. II. Corinth. XI. 3.[20]

> And when my mind hath been thus filled with care and affection, mixed with a feeling of the manifold deficulties attending business, a fresh sense of God's goodness in guiding his people [undecipherable] qualifying with sound judgement to distinguish things

that differ, and in preserving them from inward dangers, hath felt very precious to me. And thou hath often on this account been the object of my hearty desires.[21]

As I have seen that a view to live high hath been a stumbling block, and that what some appeared to aim at was no higher, than many of the foremost rank in our Society lived, there hath been a labour upon me, that in this respect, the way may be cast up, and the stumbling block taken out of the way of the people. Isaa. 57. 14. . . .

. . . Nor have I believed myself clear with out speaking at times publickly concerning it.[22]

Knowledge of worldly values and their attractiveness, and of God's values and their attractiveness, are basic pieces of knowledge if we are to discern aright. These are taught to us by our spiritual teachers and directly by our own experience of God. Having been taught by others, John Woolman sees it as his responsibility to pass on this wisdom to others. Everything is to be shared. God's graces are not meant for personal gain but for the enrichment of the people of God. Such is the definition of charism, that which is given by God to be used for others.

How few amongst the young men live in self denial, and manifest true heavenly mindedness; and I was careful for thee, that thou when looking towards them, might prize that which is most valuable and understand that the nearest approach to pure celestial happiness is the furthest distance from the ways and spirit of this world.[23]

John Woolman gave himself over to the communal discernment of his faith community. There are many examples in his letters of him being faithful to the editing process on his essays.

And if thou can feel liberty from thy other concerns, and freedom to Spend some time in a deliberate reviewing and correcting of it, and make such alterations or additions as thou believes may be usefull, the prospect of it is agreeable to me.[24]

Having thus hinted what I had thought, I am free to leave it to friends, either to omit printing them, or to print as many as to you may appear best.

With love to thee and family I remain thy loveing fr'd,
John Woolman.[25]

Belovd friends –

As I have under an apprehension of duty wrote Consideration on the true harmony of mankind and how it is to be maintained, the piece has been inspected by the Overseers of the press and by them agreed to be printed.[26]

He also desires that others act from a state of freedom. In the case of J. C., who had offered to supply him with some healing herbs, John Woolman wants to be sure that J. C. is free and not spirituality burdened.

Beloved Fr'd
I recd thy letter about a week ago, and having thought some about those herbs mentioned therein I know nothing better at present for me than to write a letter to inform thee, if thou gets it, that if thou art free to get those herbs and prepare electuary, or otherwise to procure it as thou may feel most freedom, I think at present that when it comes to hand, if it come, I may be free to take some, and to account to thee for it.[27]

In June of 1763, John Woolman was on a journey to visit native Americans (Indians). He tells in such human fashion in the journal of a night he spent in great agony of mind as to whether he was continuing on this dangerous journey really at the guidance of the inward teacher or simply for fear of the ridicule he might receive for his cowardice if he turned back.

> I lay full of thoughts great part of the night, while my beloved companion lay and slept by me, till the Lord my gracious Father, who saw the conflicts of my soul, was pleased to give quietness. Then was I again strengthened to commit my life and all things relating thereto into his heavenly hands; and getting a little sleep toward day, when morning came we rose.[28]

He questions his companions to be sure that they are answering God's call to them and not travelling only out of friendship to him. Benjamin Parvin decides to continue and William Lightfoot decides to head homeward.

In a letter home to Sarah, John Woolman writes:

> And as to Benjamin – His mind at present seems so Engaged that he Shews no Inclination to leave me: I have had Some weighty Conversation with Him and let him know that I am quite free to go alone if his way does not appear clear to Him.[29]

A few days later, William Lightfoot wrote to Sarah:

> Sarah Woolman
> I may hereby Inform thee that I met thy Husband at Samuel Foulk's last 3d day Evening, and in Discourse Concerning the Journey, he exprest a Close Exercise which the news of the Troubles to the Westward had brought upon him. Signifying that in Case the Journey should be attended with Danger from an Enemy, he thought he could be much easier to go alone than to be Instrumental in bringing any into danger, who had no weightier motive to undertake it than to Accompany him, and as I never had resolved on going, it seem'd most easy for me to Decline it. Tho' not much on the account of Danger, having heard these reports some

Time before without any great apprehensions of that, and am in Hopes that thy Husband & Benj. Parvin (who is gone with him), may Return safe again. I went with them about 20 Miles beyond Bethlehem and when I parted with them (which was last 6th. day Morning) they seem'd well and Cheerful.[30]

Through John Woolman's constant intentionality to discern God's desire for him and his obedience to that, he can speak of being in the right place, which is, of course, a state of freedom, creativity, energy, and spiritual authority.

I believe the present dispensation is profitable to me and I am often in care that I may be preserved in resignedness and feel for duty from one day to another.[31]

I feel quiet in my mind, believing it is the Lord's will that I should for a time be in this part of the world. I often remember you, and friends in your parts, as I pass along in this journey, and the Truth as it is Separate from all mixture.[32]

The act of discerning implies a desire to say to God, Thy will be done. By the discipline of daily prayer and reflection, we are brought to a place of clarity, though not without times of uncertainty, confusion, and inner turmoil.

Through a process of discerning, we make a statement to God and ourselves of our desire to be faithful. An open heart God never rejects but instead leads us into ever-deepening understanding of the faith-filled Way.

I am humbly Thankfull to My Gracious Father, who has brought my mind in a good degree to be resigned to him.[33]

John Woolman to Susannah Lightfoot, Sometime after 1764

In the fellowship of true & unfeigned love, that unites the hearts of the faithful in a joint communion one with another, do I dearly salute thee; even that communion that begets a sympathy in Spirit, to partake in some degree of the state of one another as Members of one body in the mystery that the World knows not of; for by this communion the members are not insensible of the state one of another, and if one member suffers, the other suffers with it; and if one rejoices or abounds the rest are rejoiced in a degree of the same abounding love; by this there is help communicated without partiality or sinister views, according to the proportion of that Love which is boundless, proceeding from God, thro' Jesus Christ, and centering in the same eternal fulness.

Thus my Dear Friend, if I may be so qualified as to be any way useful, I shall be much satisfied that I have performed that part of friendship that may be profitable to thee, with a great deal of pleasure, and judging also that I have had some experience of the various states and conditions of a christian life, & the manner of the Lord's dealings with his people. These I have learned in the deeps; & in the silence of fleshly reasonings; in the stillness where the Enemy approaches not have had to cry out in admiration with the Prophet: "how unsearchable are thy Judgments, O Lord! & thy ways past finding out!" Yet there is often a long time of suffering in hunger & thirst, in nakedness & distress, before we can come here to this stillness, to the intent that God Almighty in his infinite wisdom, may manifest his own Arm of power, which sometimes brings deliverance without any means of our own proposing.

I have often observed that he reserves entirely to himself the greatest deliverances, yet not always so, as not to make use of any means at all; but then those means appear on a just view, to have something in them so extraordinary and providential that they appear plainly to be from the first moving cause; the instrument is in some sort overlooked, tho' it is in sincerity acknowledged as the bounty of heaven, in the distribution of his providence, yet the acknowledgment does not terminate in the means or instrument, but arises in pure breathings, as a divine flame to the source and fountain of all our mercies.

Thus his Judgements are to human attainments unsearchable, & his ways (tho' ways that lead to peace) past our finding out. When he corrects, 'tis not in his sore displeasure, lest he should bring us to nothing; but by the chastisements, as of a merciful Father, He urges and draws a greater degree of obedience from his children, for it is in his love.

Our time then, is to be still, to bear all things, to endure all things, to rejoice in all things that he shall lay upon us, as knowing that thereby we may procure to ourselves the most lasting peace by being thus restored again to favour. And oh! how happy are all those that can so quietly submit in all things! & in order to this let us only consider that they are distributed to mankind in his abundant wisdom and counsel. But I freely confess and acknowledge, that there is another sort of affliction that is as bonds and imprisonments, as laying nights and days in the deeps (yea more afflicting than bonds outwardly), and the cause intirely hid from us, wherein there is a striving between Life and Death, between hope and despair, longing to be delivered, and but short glimpses of it, if at all beholding the deliverer, & at times crying out with the Prophet: "Thou hast compassed thyself about with a Cloud, that our prayers cannot pass thro'!" There appears no mediator, no High Priest before the Throne of God, he forever seems to hide His blessed countenance, and his absence is our greatest pain; for being deprived of his presence all things else yield no relief. O! then how does the Soul tremble, how does the heart faint! the tears are dried up, no vent that seems to ease the anguish of the Soul, no Balm in Gilead, no Physician there, so that we are ready to cry out, "Our bones are dried up! our hope is lost! we are cast off forever!" & with Job "O! that my grief were thro'ly weighed, & my calamaties put into the balance together; for then it would appear heavier than the Sands of the Sea; therefore my words are swallowed up!" O that I could feel so much softness in my heart as might affect mine eyes, then should I have hope; if it were the effect of contrition or consolation, it would yield me equal Joy, that my Redeemer had not quite forsaken me, nor given me up to the rage of my most cruel Enemy, but has mercy for me still in store. Thus lamenting Days and Nights when it is Day we wish for night, & when Night we desire Day; fear to be alone, & fear to be in company; we can neither read nor hear with attention, nor meditate on God with any composed devotion.

Yet let me tell thee, O my Friend! (having waded thro' these and more afflictions, that are not to be express'd) if such distress is now or has been upon thee, God is near at hand to bear up thy drooping Soul; he is ever underneath and round about thee, tho' for a while thou seest him not. And I have always found, that after these times he has appeared with abundant more lustre & glory; to teach us not to attribute anything to ourselves, nor fix our thoughts on anything less than his omnipotency.

He that has made the Sea, & prescribed bounds to the Waves thereof, saying "'hitherto shalt thou come & no further; & here shall thy proud waves be stayed;" is not to be limited by finite creatures, as the best of Men are;

& tho' the Sea may dash and foam, yet it cannot make an inundation but by the direction, or at least high sufferance of Almighty wisdom; who is not less in regard to His Children's well-being than wise in his counsels to frustrate the proudest attempts of the wicked. Wherefore by having an eye single to him at all times of tossing or fluctuation of the Mind, proceeding from what cause they will, is the most proper method of attaining to a settled state and condition.

When the disciples of our Lord were tossed on the Sea, their help was near, tho' to them Jesus seem'd asleep & undisturbed, yet his inward apprehension as God was awake, & ready to help them at their call, "Master, carest not thou that we perish?" Whereat he arose, & rebuked the Winds, & said to the Sea, "Peace, be still!" & the Wind ceased, & there was a great calm, whereupon their admiration seemed to be raised more by that signal deliverance, than by any other miracle, inasmuch as they at that time were the more immediate objects of his mercy & partook of the blessing of his powerful word; neither did they spare returning their acknowledgments by saying "What manner of Man is this, that even the Winds & the Seas obey him?"

Thus is he near when he seems most absent, ready to help in every needful time of trouble, as he is called upon in the least degree of faith (tho small as a grain of Mustard Seed) settling & quieting the Mind in his own time; sometimes before we ask, to prevent our asking; herein is fulfilled that saying of Scripture, "I was found of them that sought me not, & made manifest unto them that enquired not after me;" Sometimes he waits long, according to the strength of the sufferer, as is illustrated in the case of the importunate Widow, by his saying, "tho he bear long with them," yet always in his own time he will answer (and that is the best time) sometimes entirely unexpected by the Creature, & whether the Deliverer comes early or late, in that deliverance there is a looking back with wonder and acknowledgment to God, as Israel sang on the Banks of the Sea, saying, "The Lord is glorious in holiness, fearful in praise doing wonders;" or again, "these are thy wonderful works, O God! my soul has been brought down to the bottom of the pit, & thou hast delivered it again from the Destroyer, & hast once more set my feet in the just man's path, in the bright shining light that shall shine more and more unto the perfect Day."

In these short intervals the Soul gathers strength to ascend to her Beloved, & rejoices in her happy deliverance from bondage. And it is agreeable to the experience of many, that there is no state that produces such convincing proof of the regard of Heaven, as that wherein we are reduced to the last degree of poverty and want; to that degree that there appears nothing but confusion; the very brute Animals seem in a more desirable condition; they rove idly unemployed, & have their food prepared in season, and if they are slain, Death is to them an end of all sorrows. The Trees & the shrubs & all the species of inanimated things, seem to discover a greater beauty & display in livelier texture their great original than we; these tho' they all suffer decay in the course of nature, & by the scythe of time are soon reduced to the earth from whence they sprang; yet as they are insensible of pain, they neither can nor need cry out for succour; but Man, the noblest part of God's creation, made to adore and reverence the supreme being with sublime intellects, is of all creatures taught of God, to trust in him, to wait upon him, to be resigned to his will in all things; & if at any time he is pleased to hide his face for awhile, 'tis in order to manifest his power, & bring forth some lasting fruits of praise to himself; and more honour and dignity to the Creator by virtue of his prolific Word; for by Death is Life perfected; by staining the glory of this world, the glory of God is rendered more conspicuous; by seeing ourselves really as we are, we have a glimpse of what God is; by beholding our own emptiness, we desire to partake of his fulness by feeling our own poverty, we covet his riches; by being hungry & thirsty we have a true relish of the Bread and Water of Life; by a real sense of our own nothingness, we dare not murmur if we receive nothing; but in all states, with the Holy Apostle, learn to be content; thus God becomes all in all. And thus it is necessary that we have a spiritual assistance to distinguish times and seasons as they are in the hand of God; when we abound, not to be lifted up; when in poverty & want, not to repine too much; when afflicted, that we pray first for the spirit of prayer & supplication, that we may be directed how, & in what manner to pray: for it is not always consistent that we should have what we most desire as Creatures, but that which is most profitable for us as Christians, Believers, & Followers of Christ, who was a most perfect pattern of humility & self-denial whilst in the Flesh, who just before the offering up of His Life for the Sins of the whole World; & by having an apprehension of the greatest of all agonies, he breaths as if constrained by the most perfect weight, "O my Father, if it be possible, let this cup pass from me" but as if he checked himself adds, with submission and filial duty: "Nevertheless not as I will but as thou wilt!"

We therefore have great need to distinguish aright that in all things we may be preserved, by watching in stillness, to be renewed in strength; by virtue of the holy anointing to know what to ask, & temper our longings by a perfect submission: sometimes to ask no more than to be endued with patience and strength to bear the present affliction, that it may terminate to our advantage, & acceptance with Almighty God.

At other times when the Days of captivity are ended, & the Seed that has been oppressed is to be set at liberty, the Lord gives notice therof by causing the soul to breathe in open air, & to ascend to the Divine Majesty with an easy supplication; and an earnest, as it were resounding back upon the Soul, with Heavenly Harmony that strikes a firm belief that our prayers are heard, like the fire that fell upon Elijah's offering, & consumed the Wood, the Flesh, the Stone, & the Water. But when the emanations of this divine life are absent, which is not to be counted strange or a new thing, the enemy of Man's happiness who waits all opportunities like a restless & indefatigable Foe, to besiege, & if possible to storm & sack the whole City of God; he is then ready to make his strongest attempts, if possible to shake the foundation; but the foundation of God stands sure, having this Seal: "The Lord knows them that are his"; and them he will preserve and care for; tho' the Enemy may tempt, & raise considerable disorders & fluctuations in the Mind without any visible cause; at other times suggests into the Mind desponding thoughts, as if we should never more be regarded; but he who was a lyar & a murderer from the beginning, is so still; & as he abode not in the Truth, his Envy is raised the more particularly against all who strive to persevere aright.

But let us trust in God, who will not suffer us to be tempted above what we are able to bear, but will with the temptation also make a way to escape it; but those desponding thoughts have so much influence sometimes, that the Creature seems wholly swallowed up in them, & complains like Zion in bitterness of Soul saying, 'The Lord hath forsaken me! My God hath forgotten me!"

But He that was nearer than she was aware of & readier to help than she hoped, expostulated with her in the most affectionate & moving manner; "Can a woman forget her suckling child, that she should not have compassion on the Son of her Womb?" "Yea, she may!" No compassion is sufficient to illustrate the Love of

God! Women may become hardened & be careless of their own offspring, & be inexorable to the cries of their Children; but the Lord thy Maker, thy Husband that takes care of thee, will not forsake thee," "Thou are graven on the Palms of my Hands;" as much as to say, "to forget thee were to forget myself; to forget my Power, that made all things & upholds all things," "thy Walls of Protection are continually before me," "Thy Salvation is not out of sight, thy Redeemer is near at hand."

My dear Friend, I seem to myself to have exceeded the Bounds of a letter already, altho' I have been obliged to confine my thoughts very much, & have sent thee only a short extract of what has presented itself to my Mind, with a considerable share of warmth and sweetness; but I'll just add, that I have been deeply engaged in humble petition to Almighty God, that he may vouchsafe to draw nigh with the visitation of his pure light, & in mercy cause his brightness to appear, by removing the Cloud that hangs over the Tabernacle; & so far favour those who have no might of their own, as to guard them by his own Arm by Day & Night, gently leading those who are with young, & bearing them in his arms. Amen.

John Woolman[1]

Crucifixion

There are degrees of growth in the Christian progress, and all well meaning people are not in the same degree entered into that resignation, wherein men are crucified to the world.[1]

Calvary

They were all dismissed at that time with orders to remain in readiness, and soon after there came an account from the general that they were not likely to want them this time. It was a day of deep trial to the young men, yet the effect it appeared to have on their minds was such, that I thought I saw the kindness of Providence in it, and trust that if it should please Him to try us with further and heavier sufferings than what we have yet had, his arm will be sufficient to uphold them who really trust in Him.[2]

Crucifixion is a central facet of Christian theology and mystical reality. Although there are times in our lives when we make false crosses for ourselves, when we make burdens of tasks or incidents and turn them into inner states of negativity, God would prefer we dealt with them differently, in a more life-giving way.

But Christ does have a cross for each of us. Accepting and travelling with this cross Christ desires to give us is life-giving and leads to resurrection. But the fullness of the cross must be experienced first. There is no short-cut to resurrection.

To forward this work, the allwise God is sometimes pleased, through outward distress, to bring us near the gates of Death; That life being painful & afflicting, and the prospect of Eternity open before us, all earthly bonds may be loosened, and the mind prepared for that deep and Sacred Enstruction, which otherwise would not be received.[3]

By entering into the crucified Christ and Christ's cross for us, our false self is further stripped away, our attachment to worldly values shatters, and our intimacy with God deepens. We are presented with a view of ourselves, our life, and the world that is richer, more life-giving, and full of a joyful potential far beyond our human power to imagine.

It is important, however, that we do not romanticise the cross or imagine it to be beyond our capacity to bear. Romanticising the cross can lead us to false piety, e.g. I am suffering, so I must be holy. It may also tempt us to believe that all the troubles we encounter are cross experiences, e.g. I am suffering; this is what God wants.

In imagining the cross as too difficult for us, we retreat into a dimly lit religious life. Though difficult, the cross we are presented with matches our resources. God does not set us up to fail. God is only interested in presenting us with pathways we can walk and which will lead us closer to Her.

For as the rain and the snow come down from heaven,
and do not return there until they have watered the earth,
Making it bring forth and sprout,
Giving seed to the sower and bread to the eater,
so shall my word be that goes out from my mouth;
it shall not return to me empty,
but it shall accomplish that which I purpose,
and succeed in the thing for which I sent it.

For you shall go out in joy,
and be led back in peace;
the mountains and the hills before you
shall burst into song,
and all the trees of the field shall clap their hands.

(Isaiah 55:10–12 NRSV)

The religious journey is not a booby-trapped obstacle course which only a few can complete. The journey is for all of us, and it is different for each of us. God longs for us to be closer, to become more intimate with Her. God has a vested interest in our surrender, for God needs us. We are God's hands. God desires that we align ourselves with Her so that the full power of God's love and grace can flow through us into this place.

The crucifixion/resurrection process is, of course, cyclical. Crucifixion and resurrection are meant to be ongoing occurrences with the same cross or a new one, the same resurrection or a new one. This requires discernment to be a way of life.

God longs for our surrender. God has surrendered Herself to us. Christ has been surrendered for us. Will we surrender ourselves to God and so change the universe forever?

> I feel a pure and Holy Spirit in a weak & broken Constitution: this Spirit within me hath suffered deeply and I have born my part in the Suffering, that there may come forth a Church pure & clean like the New Jerusalem, as a Bride Adorned for her husband.[4]

In terms of changing ourselves and changing the world, who has the clearer vision, God or us? Whose view is more likely to lead to new life for all, God's or ours?

Whose power is the best resource in all circumstances, God's or our own?

> I have often looked at a life conformable to the wisdom and policy of man, where our wills have an open field to move in. And I have looked at a self denying humble life where the creature falling upon the true cornerstone is broken. This latter way of life to me appears most precious; and this day it came upon me to look

attentively towards the manners, the spirit, and disposition that appears common amongst the people, and I said in my heart, how few dwell deep enough.[5]

The Cost to John Woolman and His Family

My heart hath been often contrite since I saw you; and I now remember you with tears.[6]

My dear wife,
Though I feel in a good degree resigned in being absent from you, my heart is often tenderly Affected toward you, and even to weeping this morning, while I am about to write.[7]

John Woolman and Sarah Woolman were faithful to God's call, no matter the personal cost. It came with long periods of separation which were extremely difficult to bear. John Woolman left home faithfully but not altogether happily: *in a good degree resigned.*

It is only through his connectedness with Sarah and God, and his abandonment to God, that he had the inner strength to continue.

I am about to leave home under much thoughtfulness, & at times it seems to border upon distress of Mind. But [I] retain a desire to put my whole trust in Him who is able to help throug [sic] all troubles.[8]

The tender concern which I have many times felt for thee, and for Mary and for John, and even for Betsy, I may not easily express. I have often remembered you with tears; and my desires have been that the Lord, who hath been my helper through many Adversities, may be a Father to you, and that in his love, you may be guided Safely along.[9]

That going out at this time, when Sickness is so great
amongst you, is a tryal upon me; yet I often remember
there are many Widows and Fatherless, many who have
poor Tutors, many who have evil Examples before them,
and many whose minds are in Captivity, for whose sake
my heart is at times moved with Compassion, that I feel
my mind resigned to leave you for a Season, to exercise
that gift which the Lord hath bestowed on me, which
though small compared with some, yet in this I rejoyce,
that I feel love unfeigned toward my fellow-creatures.[10]

On his travels, he often wrote to Sarah and longed to receive
letters from her. When letters from Sarah reached him, they
encouraged and nourished him. He expressed his concern for
Sarah in his letters to friends, and he relied on them to care
for her and their daughter Mary—an example of the long
tradition of mutual support in faith communities.

I hope my dear Wife will be noticed by her friends.[11]

When we are ministering away from home, our heart is often
turned towards our family and friends at home, and our desire
is to get the work done as quickly as possible. The temptation
is to hurry. But this *is* temptation. Ministering requires time,
God's time, which may be much longer than we would
humanly like.

A little-used Quaker term is a 'necessity'. A necessity is a call
from God which requires us to change our life. The call is
insistent, and we cannot lay it down. It is as pressing as
breathing. The option of saying No is so remote that we can
do no other than say Yes, despite the price that will be
incurred.

Only God can remove a necessity from our ministry.

I hear by Wm. Lightfoot thou hast been poorly but at
the time of his passing by was better. Thy not
mentioning it in thy letters, I consider as intended

kindness to me by forbearing to contribute to the Increase of my Exercise. I feel a most tender Concern for thee, as knowing thy Condition to be Attended with dificulty, and find at times a disposition to hasten for thy Sake. But Such is the weight of the work I am engaged in, and Such the baptisms with which I have been baptized; that I see A Necessity for all nature to Stand Silent. I know not that I ever have had a Sharper Conflict in Spirit, or better understood what it was to take up the Cross, than of late. The depth of which Exercise is know (sic) only to the Almighty, and yet my beloved companion Saml. [Samuel Eastburn] hath been a true and faithful Sympathizer with me.[12]

John Woolman Accepts the Cross

We have been fellow feelers with the afflicted nor is any affliction too great to endure for the Truth.[13]

Our Journey though attended with much deep Exercise hath been greatly to our Satisfaction.[14]

John Woolman knows well the difficulty of being faithful, but he recognises that God's inner presence is the *most* delightful and the *most* pure experience and that those who have turned towards God will be able to find their consolation, even in times of difficulty. Whilst he has this deep knowledge of consolation, the ministry given to John Woolman taxes him and is not easy.

My heart hath been often melted into contrition since I left thee, under a Sence of divine goodness being extended for my help and preparing in me a Subjection to his will.[15]

As the present appearance of things is not joyous, I have been much shut up from outward Chearfulness, remembering that promise, "Then shalt thou delight thyself in the Lord." As this from day to day has been revived in my memory, I have considered that his Internal presence on our minds is a delight of all others the most pure; and that the honest hearted not only delight in this, but in the Effect of it upon them. He regards the helpless and distressed, and reveals his Love to His Children under Affliction.[16]

A fundamental part of our openness is to be truthful to God, to honestly say how we are finding our journey, i.e. to say what is. As we enter more deeply into the reality of our experience, God is more able to teach and sustain us. Denying the truth of ourselves puts up barriers that inhibit our receptivity to the Spirit.

Looking seriously over the stages and wide waters and thinking on the hard frosts and high winds usual in the winter, the journey has appeared difficult; but my mind was turned to him, who made and commands the winds and the waters, and whose providence is over the ravens and the sparrows.[17]

Mutual relationship in community and in our ministry supports us through the shared experience, forming deeper relationships that strengthen us in difficult times.

As I was lately transcribing some notes I made in the southern parts when thee and I were there together, my mind was brought to feel over again some heavy labours which I believe we had both some share of, and to desire we might ever attend to Him whose fatherly regard was extended toward us in that lonely journey.[18]

John Woolman paid a price for his obedience to God's will, and while he shared of this with friends, and particularly with Sarah, only God knows the full price he paid. Yet, through his obedience and trials his relationship with God grew. His letters are full of his thanksgiving for the graces God has bestowed on him.

I am not so hearty and healthy as I have been Sometimes, and yet through the Mercy of the Almighty I am enabled to persue our Journey without much difficulty on that Account.[19]

Concern for Others' Ministries

As is usual with John Woolman, from his experience of being attentive to God's call in himself he encourages and supports others in their ministries. He urges them to linger when necessary, to give themselves into God's time, and to take the opportunities that are presented to them to minister, however inauspicious the circumstances may appear. From his own experience, he is sympathetic to the cost they are paying to follow God.

> Since I understand thy draft toward New England at this season of the year, I have felt a near sympathy in my mind toward thee, and also thy new companion, H. White. . . .

> . . . Should frozen rivers or high winds or storms sometimes prevent thy going forward so fast as thou could desire, it may be thou may find a service in tarrying even amongst a people whose company may not be every way agreeable. I remembered that the manner in which Paul made a visit to the island of Melita was contrary to his own mind as a man; we find, however, that by means thereof, the father of Publius was healed of his fever, and many cured of their infirmities.[20]

Into the Rose Garden

We have had the courage to walk down the corridor accepting God's love, accepting our brokenness, accepting God's healing power. We have accepted the invitation to be obedient and have faithfully discerned our call.

What do we find when we open the door and enter the rose garden? The landscape is full of God's blessings, the roses are blooming, and a heavenly scent fills the air. But not all the flower heads are in bloom. Some are dead, and the rose bushes have thorns which draw blood.

There is always a price to pay in being faithful. At times the price is invisible as our vision is full of the love and grace of God working through us. At other times there is distress when the fruits of the work are beyond our knowing, and we ask, Are we wasting our time? These are times when we feel the inevitable loneliness in our ministry.

On other occasions, the cost seems too high. We may struggle, we may doubt, but with perseverance and grace we are still able to say Yes.

> We may see ourselves cripled and halting, & from a strong bias to things pleasant and easie, find an Impossibility to advance forward.[21]

> Our visits in general have hitherto been in weakness, and to me it hath been a time of abasement. I hope, notwithstanding, our appointing meetings have not been to the dishonour of Truth.[22]

> My dear and tender wife
> A Sence of Alsufficiency of God in Supporting those who trust in Him in all the Dispensations of His Providence wherein they may be tryed feels comfortable to me in my Journey.[23]

Letters: April 1772 to September 1772

15 April 1772, to Israel Pemberton

Beloved Friend

Thine by J. Comfort came to hand. It would be agreeable to my mind that the piece beef handed to James, & if no objection arise, to its being after opened to the Meeting for Sufferings that it be also opened there.

As my mind hath been more particularly drawn toward the northern parts of England, I do not yet feel Setled to sail for London; but know not what may be as to that.

thy loving frd.

John Woolman.[1]

April 1772, to Israel Pemberton

Beloved friend

I believe I may endeavour to see Joseph White soon. If thou and Such in this City who are careful to look over writings proposd to be printed, and to amend what may be imperfect, would employ a little time in correcting that piece, and afterwards let me see the prepard alterations, it would be acceptable to me to look over them.

Though I know not how it may be as to the sailing in this Vessel, I am in care to Endeavour to be in readiness soon.

Seventh day morning.   John Woolman.[2]

28 April 1772, to Elizabeth Smith

Beloved Sister, – I have often had a tender feeling with thee in thy outward afflictions, and I trust, in some measure, with thee in thy inward exercises. I believe our afflictions are often permitted by our heavenly Father for our more full and perfect refining.

The Truth my dear sister, hath been precious in thy sight, and I trust remains to be to thee precious as ever.

In the pure and undefiled way, that which is not of the Father, but of the world, is purged out.

Christ of old time taught the people as they were able to bear it, and I believe, my dear friend, there are lessons for thee and me yet to learn. Friends from the country and in the city, are often at thy house, and when they behold amongst thy furniture some things which are not agreeable to the purity of Truth, the minds of some, I believe at times, are in danger of being diverted from so close an attention to the Light of life as is necessary for us.

I believe, my dear friend, the Lord hath weaned thy mind in a great measure, from all these things, and when I signed thy certificate, expressing thee to be exemplary, I had regard to the state of thy mind as it appeared to me; but many times since I signed it, I felt a desire to open to thee a reserve which I then, and since often felt, as to the exemplariness of those things amongst thy furniture which are against the purity of our principles.

I trust the Great Friend and Helper is near thee, in whose love I am thy friend,

John Woolman.

I desired my wife to keep this letter for thee when she might see thee.[3]

28 April 1772, to John and Mary Comfort, daughter and son-in-law

Dear Children:

I feel a tender care for you at this time of parting from you, and under this care, my mind is turned toward the pure Light of Truth, to which if you take diligent heed I trust you will find inward Support under all your trials.

My leaving you under the trying Circumstances now attending you, is not without close exercise and I feel a living concern, that under these cares of business, and under bodily affliction, your minds may be brought to a humble waiting on Him who is the great Preserver of his people. Your loving parent

John Woolman.[4]

13 June 1772, to Sarah Woolman

Dear Wife

Through the mercies of the Lord I arived safe in London on the 8 da. 6mo. I was mercifully helped to bear the difficulties of the Sea, and went strait from the water Side into the yearly meeting of ministers and elders after it was Setled in the morning: And the meeting of business was first opened the same day in the Afternoon. My heart hath been often melted into contrition since I left thee, under a Sence of divine goodness being extended for my help and preparing in me a Subjection to his will. I have been comforted in the company of some Sincere hearted Friends. The yearly meeting of business ended about three hours ago, and I have thoughts of going in a few days out of this Citty towards Yorkshire: taking some meetings in my way, if Strengthened thereto.

The tender concern which I have many times felt for thee, and for Mary and for John, and even for Betsy, I may not easily express. I have often remembered you with tears; and my desires have been that the Lord, who hath been my helper through many Adversities, may be a Father to you, and that in his love, you may be guided Safely along.

Rob. Willis, Sarah Morris and Companion, W. Hunt & Companion,, and S. Emlen, all here and midling well. Robert, going, I expect, for Ireland, and W. Hunt & compan[io]n, I expect, for Holland. Several friends remembr. kind love to thee. My kind love is to my dear friends.

John Woolman.[5]

14 June 1772, to Reuben and Margaret Haines

Cousins Reuben and Margaret,

I am middling well, in London, and believe I may go northward in a few days. Your care for me toward parting hath felt inwardly gathering toward the true union in which I hope we may at last unite.

My heart hath been often contrite since I saw you; and I now remember you with tears.

John Woolman

My friend Suse, and my little cousins, I remember you all.[6]

14 June 1772, to John Woolman Jr., son of John Woolman's brother Abner

I have often felt tender desires that my cousin, John Woolman, may be preserved in a watchful frame of mind, and know that which supports innocent young people against the snares of the Wicked.

The deep Tryals of thy Father and his inward care for you are often in my remembrance, with some Concern that you, his children, may be acquainted with that inward life to which his mind, whilst among us, was often gathered.

John Woolman.[7]

19 June 1772, to John Townsend

Beloved friend John Townsend, if any letter comes to thy hand directed to me, I desire thou may open it in private, and Shew it to no one, and if thou believes it to be of a nature greatly requiring haste, then send it by the post, else keep it till other oportunity of conveyance thy loving friend

John Woolman

I am now at baldock near as well as when I left London 19 day 6 mo. 1772

Joseph Roe is desired to give this to John Townsend.[8]

31 July 1772, to John Townsend

Beloved Friend:

I am now at John Haslam's on the edge of Yorkshire, midling well in health. Sarah Morris and her companion were midling well here yesterday. If thou will keep the within letter until thou hast convenient opportunity to send it, it will be acceptable to me. I feel contented as to hearing from the family I left in America.

With true love to thee and thy wife and children

I remain thy frd.

John Woolman.[9]

31 July 1772, to Sarah Woolman

My dear wife,

Though I feel in a good degree resigned in being absent from you, my heart is often tenderly Affected toward you, and even to weeping this morning, while I am about to write.

The numerous difficulties attending us in this life are often before me, and I often remember thee with tender desires that the holy Spirit may be thy leader, and my leader through life, and that at last we may enter into rest.

My journey hath been through inward watchfulness, I see but a little way at a time, but the Lord hath been gracious to me, and way opens for my Visit in these parts.

Thy loving Husband

John Woolman.

about 160 miles northward from London[10]

31 July 1772, to Reuben and Margaret Haines

Beloved Cousins,

I am now at our ancient Friend, John Haslam's, whose memory is much impaired by the palsy; but he appears to be in a meek, quiet state; about one hundred and sixty miles northward of London. My journeying hath been through much inward watchfulness. I cannot see far before me. But the Lord, in tender mercy, hath been gracious to me, and way opens for my visit among Friends.

Friends from America, on visits here, were all midling well lately.

I send no letters by post here, nor do I want any sent to me by post.

I feel a care that we humbly follow the pure leadings of Truth, and then, I trust, all will work for good.

Your loving cousin,

John Woolman[11]

30 August 1772, to Rachel Wilson

30: 8: 1772

This morning I wrote a letter in substance as follows

Beloved friend,

My mind is often affected as I pass along under a sense of the state of many poor people, who sit under that sort of ministry which requires much outward labour to support it; And the loving kindness of our heavenly Father in opening a pure gospel Ministry in this nation hath often raised thankfulness in my heart toward Him. I often remember the Conflicts of the faithful under persecution, and now look at the free exercise of the pure gift uninterrupted by outward laws as a trust committed to us, which requires our deepest gratitude, and most careful attention. I feel a tender concern that the work of reformation so prosperously carried on in this land within a few ages past may go forward and spread amongst the nations, and may not go backward through dust gathering on our garments, who have been called to a work so great and so precious.

Last evening I had a little opportunity at thy house, with some of thy family in thy absence, in which I rejoyced, and feeling a Sweetness on my mind toward thee I now endeavour to open a little of the feeling I had there.

I have heard that you in these parts have, at certain seasons, meetings of Conferrence, in relation to friends living up to our principles, in which several meetings unite in one, with which I feel unity: I having in some measure felt Truth lead that way amongst friends in America; and have found my dear friend, that, in these labours, all Superfluities in our own living are against us. I feel that pure love toward thee in which there is freedom.

I look at that precious gift bestowed on thee, with Awfulness before Him who gave it and feel a care that we may be so Separated to the gospel of Christ that those things which proceed from the Spirit of this world may have no place amongst us. thy frd

John Woolman[12]

I commit this letter to the hands of Our ancient friend at greyrig meeting, at whose house I write with desire for him not to send it to thee, but keep it laid by till he hath oportunity to give it to thee.

I have sent no letter by post in England, and if thou feels a Concern to write to me and art easie to wait an opportunity of conveyance Some other way than post or flying Coaches I believe it would be most acceptable

J.W.

flying Coaches I mean those coaches which run so fast as oft to oppress the horses.[13]

16 September 1772, to John and Mary Comfort

To the children of Stephen Comfort of Bucks County.

I am now, this 16th 9th, 1772, at Robert Proud's in Yorkshire, so well as to continue travelling, though but slowly.

Yesterday, as I was walking over a plain on my way to this place, I felt a degree of Divine love attend my mind, and therein an openness toward the children of Stephen

Comfort, of which I believed I should endeavour to inform them. My mind was opened to behold the happiness, the safety and beauty of a life devoted to follow the heavenly Shepherd; and a care that the enticements of vain young people may not ensnare any of you.

I cannot form a concern, but when a concern cometh, I endeavour to be obedient.

John Woolman.[14]

22 September 1772, to John Wilson

Beloved Friend

When I followed the Trade of a Tailor, I had a feeling of that which pleased the proud mind in people; & growing uneasie, was strengthened to leave off that which was superfluous in my Trade.

When I was at your house, I believe I had a sense of the pride of people being gratified in some of the business thou followest, and feel a concern in pure love to endeavour to inform thee of it.

Christ our leader is worthy of being followed in his leadings at all times. The enemy gets many on his side.

O! that we may not be divided between the two, but may be wholly on the side of Christ.

In true love to you all I remain thy friend

John Woolman.[15]

23 September 1772, to John Woolman's cousins Reuben and Margaret Haines

This is John Woolman's last letter, as far as we know, written a day or two before he was taken ill of smallpox, of which he died.

Beloved Cousins: – I am now at york at a quarterly meeting. 23: mo 9: 72 So well in health as to continue travelling I appoint a few meetings, but not so fast as I did some time ago. I feel quiet in my mind, believing it is the Lord's will that I should for a time be in this part of the world. I often remember you, and friends in your parts, as I pass along in this journey, and the Truth as it is Separate from all mixture. The Truth as it is in Jesus was never more precious to me than I feel it in this my s Sojourning; in which my mind is often deeply affected with that which is not of the Father but of the world. I hear that dear W. Hunt departed this life with the small pox 9: 9: 72 and that some of his last words were The Truth Is Over All. The rest of the America friends on the visit were lately living, and mostly midling well so far as I hear.

I left my bed and Some things on board the ship I came in, directing the people to convey them to you if they arive safe at philada [Philadelphia].

John Woolman.[16]

Deliverance from Bondage

[A]s Israel sang on the Banks of the Sea, saying, "The Lord is glorious in holiness, fearful in praise doing wonders;" or again, "these are thy wonderful works, O God! my soul has been brought down to the bottom of the pit, & thou hast delivered it again from the Destroyer, & hast once more set my feet in the just man's path, in the bright shining light that shall shine more and more unto the perfect Day."[1]

Through love, God invites us to live a resurrected life here on Earth prior to our resurrection into eternal life. We reach the fertile valley, and a highway shall be there, and it shall be called the Sacred Way (Isaiah 35 NJB), and we find our hearts desiring to stay constantly focused on God. We see more clearly what is life-giving. We recognise how little we can do, how great is God's power, and how much God can do through us when we cooperate. We find our eyes opened, as if we had been blind, to the reality of God's presence in our lives, in our past and in our present. Our journey takes on an added importance and meaning. We understand so much and realise how little that is. We are in awe.

And I have always found, that after these times he has appeared with abundant more lustre & glory; to teach us not to attribute anything to ourselves, nor fix our thoughts on anything less than his omnipotency.[2]

Through the wisdom we learn in the Silence, we are overcome by the holiness of God, and though, in our humility, we resist calling ourselves holy or saintly, we have entered into that journey which leads to total intimacy with God.

125

We value even more the friendship of a God-centred person, one who is spiritually mature, experienced in the ways of God, and able to recognise patterns in the spiritual journey.

This deliverance from Calvary is God's gift to us and arrives mysteriously. We recognise it and receive it as the result of living a discerning life.

> And judging also that I have had some experience of the various states and conditions of a christian life, & the manner of the Lord's dealings with his people. These I have learned in the deeps; & in the silence of fleshly reasonings; in the stillness where the Enemy approaches not have had to cry out in admiration with the Prophet: "how unsearchable are thy Judgments, O Lord! & thy ways past finding out!" Yet there is often a long time of suffering in hunger & thirst, in nakedness & distress, before we can come here to this stillness, to the intent that God Almighty in his infinite wisdom, may manifest his own Arm of power, which sometimes brings deliverance without any means of our own proposing.[3]

The following is an extract from my 1998 retreat journal:

> I am standing outside the empty tomb weeping and wailing. There are two angels in the tomb, and they ask me why I am weeping.

> "Because they have taken the body of my master away."

> I want to go into the tomb but can't. There is someone else in the tomb, and He speaks to me.

> "Why are you weeping?"

> "If you know where they have taken Him, please tell me."

> I am standing with my back to this other person when He says, "Mary."

I go cold with shock that quickly fills with joy. It is my Christ. I whirl round and throw myself at his feet. He lifts me up.

"I still have work to do, Mary. Will you tell my brothers and sisters that I live?"

"Yes, my Lord."

The tomb is now ten times as big. The angels float up to the ceiling with Jesus between them.

Jesus says, "You are full of my seed."

The ceiling expands and becomes the universe, full of stars and music from the heavenly choir singing all into union with God.

John Woolman wrote:
> The prospect of Eternity open before us, all earthly bonds may be loosened, and the mind prepared for that deep and Sacred Instruction, which otherwise would not be received. . . .
> . . . Do we pass through it with anguish and great bitterness, & yet recover?[4]

We have wept, doubted, and, gradually, have spoken the life-giving words "Thy will be done." After a time of gestation in the tomb, God raises us into new life. We are, indeed, born again. We may look the same to others. Our actions may appear the same. To all outward appearances, nothing may have changed, but we have been transformed and are living in a state of deeper union with God. We have been imbued with a greater love for others, and in our ministry we will humbly and anonymously work as outlets for the power of God in ways unimaginable beforehand. If we are willing, this grace may be received each day, early in life and close to death. At all stages of our life, God is desiring to raise us up, to set us free.

In these short intervals the Soul gathers strength to ascend to her Beloved, & rejoices in her happy deliverance from bondage.[5]

The transforming action of the hand of God prepares us for a deeper level of awareness of others. This transformation is a gift that God desires to bear fruit in our ministry. At times, this will be affected through the presence of our transformed selves standing on a street corner with the Love of God flowing through us to the strangers passing by. On other occasions, our new ministry will be more direct.

> In this thy late affliction I've found a deep fellow-feeling with thee, and had a secret hope throughout that it might please the Father of Mercies to raise thee up.[6]
> I dearly salute thee; even that communion that begets a sympathy in Spirit, to partake in some degree of the state of one another as Members of one body in the mystery that the World knows not of.[7]

The great mystery of the wisdom of God blesses us. We are surprised by a revelation that is beyond our effort. Indeed, God bypasses our effort.

We look for something, and out of the blue we are given something else. God knows what we need better than we do. We travel to reach the point where we stop pushing and concentrate on receiving in a state of being still, untarnished by the anxiety of searching.

God constantly has to cut through our illusions, our empty desires, our blindness and interior noise, to lead us to that state of abandonment to God's wisdom in which the resurrected life can be lived.

Our soul is set aflame. We float above the ground, tingling, in awe, singing God's praises. We recognise that each breath comes from God. From our hearts is elicited voices singing God's praise and the desire to accept the invitation to sainthood, that state of being overwhelmed by God's holiness where God is the centre of all of our life, our husband, wife, brother, sister, lover, healer, teacher, and friend.

> Thus his Judgements are to human attainments unsearchable, & his ways (tho' ways that lead to peace) past our finding out. When he corrects, 'tis not in his sore displeasure, lest he should bring us to nothing; but by the chastisements, as of a merciful Father, He urges and draws a greater degree of obedience from his children, for it is in his love.[8]

We enter a state of peacefulness that imbues our very being with an awareness of what is life-giving, and we desire to grow.

> Our time then, is to be still, to bear all things, to endure all things, to rejoice in all things that he shall lay upon us, as knowing that thereby we may procure to ourselves the most lasting peace by being thus restored again to favour. And oh! how happy are all those that can so quietly submit in all things! & in order to this let us only consider that they are distributed to mankind in his abundant wisdom and counsel. . . .

> At other times when the Days of captivity are ended, & the Seed that has been oppressed is to be set at liberty, the Lord gives notice therof by causing the soul to breathe in open air, & to ascend to the Divine Majesty with an easy supplication; and an earnest, as it were resounding back upon the Soul, with Heavenly Harmony that strikes a firm belief that our prayers are heard, like the fire that fell upon Elijah's offering, & consumed the Wood, the Flesh, the Stone, & the Water.[9]

William Tuke to Reuben Haines, 26 October 1772

Dear Friend Reuben Haines,

It falls to my lot, in the fullfilling of the previous request of our beloved friend, John Woolman, hereby to inform thee that he departed this life, at the house of our friend Thomas Priestman, in the suburbs of this city, the 7th day of the 10th month 1772, about the sixth hour in the morning, and was interred in Friends' burying-ground here, the 9th of the same, after a large and solid meeting, held on the occasion in our great meeting house.

He came to this city the 21st of the ninth month, and second day of the week, having been poorly in health for some time before; apprehended the like feverish disorder he usually had at this season of the year was coming upon him.

The Quarterly meeting of Ministers and Elders was held in the evening of 3d day, and the sittings of the Quarterly meeting for Business meetings for Worship on the 4th & 5th days, all which he was enabled to attend, except the parting meeting for Worship.

He appeared in the Ministry [at our Quarterly Meeting] greatly to the comfort and satisfaction of Friends; the Spring of the Gospel flowing through him with great purity & Sweetness. His last Testimony was in a Meeting for Discipline, on the Subject of the Slave Trade: remarking, that as Friends had been solicitous for, and obtain'd relief from many of their Sufferings, so he recommended this oppressed part of the Creation to their Notice, that they may, in an Individual Capacity, as way may open, remonstrate their hardships &

Sufferings to those in Authority, especially the Legislative Power in this Kingdom. (I am persuaded that this his last public labour made a deep impression on many minds, and I wish the great sufferings he hath passed through, on account of this oppressed and injured people, may deeply affect the minds of those in America, among whom he hath faithfully and painfully laboured, and of whom he said he was clear.)

His Illness growing upon him, some Spotts appeared upon his Face like the small Pox on 7th day, & the next day it appeared beyond a doubt that this was his disorder. As he had seldom eaten Flesh for some Time, and from the Symptoms at first, we entertained hopes he would have the disorder favourably; but a great quantity of Spotts began to appear the 3rd & 4th days, so that he was pretty full, and though not so loaded as many, yet for the most part was greatly afflicted, but bore it with the utmost Meekness, Patience, Resignation and Christian Fortitude frequently uttering many comfortable & Instructive Expressions, some of which were minuted down or remembered. (Nothing was wanting that could be devised to make him easy, and to have restored him, had it been consistent with the Divine will.)

The Friend and his wife at whose house he was, as well as divers others of us, being nearly united to him in much tenderness of Affection and near Sympathy, thought it a blessing to have the opportunity of attending him, to behold his exemplary conduct, which appeared throughout. My Wife and I were much with him, both of us seldom leaving him at once, either Day or Night, as it was his Request about a Week before his death that she would not sleep out of the House till she saw an Alteration, which we freely complied with, and neither of us lodged at Home from that time.

(In the beginning of his Illness he expressed a desire to see his Neighbour and shipmate, John Bispham, and an

Opportunity offering of sending Word, to his and our Satisfaction he came, about two days before his Decease, and stayed till after the Funeral.

It seemed according to a natural probability, that the Malignancy of the Disorder was not so great but he might Survive it; [but seemed to] lay in his Constitution being so enfeebled as not to be able to struggle through, the putrid state of the latter part of the Disease: which appeared to be the Case: for about eight hours before his Departure, the Fever (which had not been immoderate) left him, and Nature sunk under its Load.

In the Forepart of his Illness, he gave Directions concerning his Papers and Funeral with the same Ease and Composure as if going a journey, and during the whole time, his Understanding was wonderfully preserved clear and sound, and his Mind so Supported in Stillness, patience, resignation and fortitude, as made it very edifying and instructing to be with him.)

First day, 27th of 9th mo. Being asked to have the advice of a Doctor he signified he had not liberty in his Mind so to do, standing wholly resigned to his Will who gave him Life, and whose Power he had witnessed to heal him in Sickness before, when he seemed nigh unto Death; and if he was to wind up now, he was perfectly resigned, having no Will either to live or die, and did not choose any should be sent for to him; but a Young Man of our Society, an Apothecary, coming of his own accord the next day, & desiring to do something for him, he said he found freedom to confer with him & the other Friends about him, and if any thing should be proposed as to Medicine that did not come through defiled Channels or oppressive Hands, he should be willing to consider and take it so far as he found freedom.

The next day he said he felt the Disorder affect his Head, so that he could think little & but as a child, & desired, if his Understanding should be more affected, to have nothing given him that those about him knew he had a Testimony against.

The same day. He desired a friend to write, and brake forth as follows: "O Lord my God! the amazing Horrors of Darkness were gathered around me, and Covered me all over, and I saw no way to go forth. I felt the depth & extent of the Misery of my fellow Creatures, separated from the Divine Harmony; and it was heavier than I could bear, and I was crushed down under it. I lifted up my hand, and I stretched out my Arm, but there was none to help me; I looked round about, and was amazed in the depths of Misery. O Lord! I remembered that thou art Omnipotent; that I had called thee Father, and I felt that I loved thee; and I was made quiet in thy Will, and I waited for Deliverance from thee; Thou hadst pity upon me when no Man could help me; I saw that Meekness under Suffering, was showed unto us, in the most affecting example of thy Son, and thou wast teaching me to follow Him; and I said, thy will, O Father, be done."

4th day morning, being asked how he felt himself, he meekly answered, "I don't know that I [. . .] slept this Night. I feel the Disorder making its progress; but my Mind is mercifully preserved in stillness & Peace." Some time after, he said he was sensible the pains of Death must be hard to bear, but if he escaped them now, he must sometime pass through them, and did not know he could be better prepared, but he had no Will in it. He said he had settled his outward affairs to his own Mind, had taken leave of his Wife & Family as never to return, leaving them to the Divine protection; adding, "and though I feel them near to me at this Time, yet I freely give them up, having a hope they will be provided for;" and a little after, said, "This trial is made easier than I could have thought, by my Will being wholly taken away; for if I was anxious as to the Event, it would be harder; but I am not, and my mind enjoys a perfect calm."

At another Time, he said, he was a little uneasy lest any should think he had put himself into the hands of the Young Man and another Apothecary who of their own choice attended him; and desired Friends might be informed, & he would inform the young man, upon what bottom they attended him, being of the same Judgment his Friends in America and some here knew he had been of; but that he found a freedom to confer with them, finding Nature needed Support, during the Time permitted to struggle with the disorder; that he had no Objection to use the Things in the Creation for real Use, & in their proper places; but anything that came through defiled Channels or Oppressive Hands, he could not touch with; having had a Testimony to bear against those things, which he hoped to bear to the last.

He lay for a considerable time in a Still, sweet frame; uttering many broken expressions, part of which were thus; "My Soul is poured out unto thee like Water, and my Bones are out of joint. I saw a Vision, in which I beheld the great Confusion of those that depart from thee. I saw their Horror & great distress. I was made sensible of their Misery, then was I greatly distressed; I looked unto thee; thou wast underneath & supported me. I likewise saw the great Calamity that is coming upon this disobedient Nation."

In the Night, a young woman having given him something to drink, he said, "My child! thou seemest very kind to me a poor Creature, the Lord will reward thee for it." A while after he cried out with great earnestness of Spirit, "O my Father, my Father!" and soon after he said, "O my Father, my Father! How comfortable art thou to my Soul in this trying season!"

Being ask'd if he could take a little Nourishment, after some pause, he replied, "My child, I cannot tell what to say to it; I seem nearly arrived where my Soul shall have rest from all its troubles."

After giving in something to be put into his Journal he said, "I believe the Lord will now excuse me from Exercises of this kind, and I see now no Work but one, which is to be the last wrought by me in this World; the Messenger will come that will relieve me from all these troubles, but it must be in the Lord's Time, which I am waiting for. I have laboured to do whatever was required according to the Ability received, in the remembrance of which I have peace; and though the disorder is strong at Times and would come over my Mind like a Whirlwind yet it has hitherto been kept steady and centred in Everlasting Love, and if that is mercifully continued, I ask nor desire more." . . .

At another Time said, he had long had a View of visiting this Nation & some time before he came, had a Dream in which he saw himself in the Northern parts of it; & that the Spring of the Gospel was opened in him, much as in the beginning of Friends, such as George Fox and William Dewsbury; and he saw the different States of the People as clear as he have ever seen Flowers in a Garden; but in his going on, he was suddenly stopt, though he could not see for what End; but looking towards home, he thereupon fell into a flood of Tears which waked him. At another time he said, "My Draught seemed strongest to the North, and I mentioned in my own Monthly Meeting that attending the Quarterly meeting at York, & being there, looked like home to me."

5th day night. Having repeatedly consented to take a Medicine with a View to settle his Stomach, but without Effect; the friend then waiting on him said, through Distress, "What shall I do now?" He answered with great Composure, "Rejoice evermore, and in everything give thanks": but added a little after, "This is sometimes hard to come at."

6th day morning, early. He brake forth in supplication in this wise; "O Lord! it was thy Power that enabled me to forsake Sin in my Youth, and I have felt thy Bruises since for disobedience, but as I bowed under them, thou healest me; and though I have gone through many Trials and sore Afflictions, thou hast been with me, continuing a Father and a Friend. I feel thy Power now, and beg that in the approaching trying Moments, thou wilt keep my Heart stedfast unto thee"

Upon giving the same Friend Directions concerning some little things, she said, I will take care, but hope thou mayst live to order them thyself; he replied, "My hope is in Christ; and though I may now seem a little better, a change in the Disorder may soon happen and my little Strength be dissolved; and if it so happen, I shall be gather'd to my everlasting Rest." On her saying she did not doubt that, but could not help Mourning to see so many faithful Servants removed at so low a Time, he said, "All good cometh from the Lord, whose Power is the same and can work as he sees best."

The same day, after giving her directions about wrapping his Corps, and perceiving her to Weep, he said, "I had rather thou wouldest guard against Weeping and sorrowing for me, my Sister; I sorrow not, though I have had some painful Conflicts; but now they seem over, and Matters all settled; and I look at the Face of my Dear Redeemer, for Sweet is his Voice and his countanance Comely."

1st day, 4th of 10 mo. Being very week, and in general difficult to be understood, he uttered a few Words in commemoration of the Lord's Goodness to him, and added; "How tenderly have I been waited on in this Time of Affliction, in which I may say in Job's words, Tedious days and wearisome Nights are appointed to me; and how many are spending their Time and Money in Vanity & Superfluities, while Thousands and Tens of

Thousands want the Necessaries of Life, who might be relieved by them, and their distress at such a Time as this, in some degree softened by their ministering of suitable things."

2nd day morning. The Apothecary not in profession with us who also appeared very anxious to assist him being present, he queried about the probability of such a Load of Matter being thrown off his weak Body. And the Apothecary making some remarks, implying he thought it might; he spoke with an Audible Voice on this wise: "My Dependence is on the Lord Jesus Christ, who I trust will forgive my Sins, which is all I hope for; and if it be his Will to raise up this Body again, I am content; and if to die, I am resigned; and if thou canst not be easy without trying to assist Nature in order to lengthen out my Life, I submit."

After this, his throat was so much affected that it was very difficult for him to speak so as to be understood, & he frequently wrote, though blind, when he wanted anything.

About the 2nd hour on 4th day morning he asked for Pen and Ink, and at several times with much difficulty wrote thus: "I believe my being here is in the Wisdom of Christ; I know not as to Life or Death." About a quarter before Six the same Morning, he seemed to fall into an easy sleep, which continued about half an Hour; when seeming to awake, he breathed a few Times with a little more difficulty, & so expired without Sigh, Groan or Struggle.

Thus this (Patient & faithful Servant of the Lord) finished (a Life of deep exercise & many Sorrows.) May the consideration of his extraordinary faithfulness, and devotedness to do whatsoever he believed his duty, excite those who survive him to diligence in doing or suffering whatsoever may be required of them; so would the many obvious inconsistencies amongst us as a people be removed, and the great work of reformation go forward and prosper in the earth. . . .

My dear love to those few in America to whom I am personally known and to all who love the Truth unto whom this may come.

With the salutation of true brotherly love I conclude, and remain thy sincere friend,

William Tuke

(P.S. Our friend J. Woolman enquired what kind of Coffins are mostly used by Friends here? how the Corps are usually wrapped, &c. and the expense? I told him Friends would be very willing to bear those charges, in case of his Decease; but he was not easy they should, and therefore, after some consideration, ordered me to write the inclosed, which he signed, and said I might send to thee: giving his Clothes to defray the Expenses of his Funeral.

He was not willing to have the Coffin made of Oak, because it is a wood more useful than ash for some other purposes.

I gave the carpenter some part of his Clothes, which I thought equal to the value of the coffin; as also some other part to a friend for flannel; but they seeming to prefer Money, John Bispham gave them to the value, and has ordered the Clothes to be sent to America, with the rest of what belonged to him. [They have been hung in the air a considerable time lest they should retain the infection, and are intended to be sent in a box with some leather from Thomas Priestman for Benjamin Mason and John Bispham.] His shoes were given to the Grave-digger.)

W. T.[1]

An ash coffin made plain without any manner of superfluities, the corpse to be wrapped in cheap flannel, the expense of which I leave my wearing clothes to defray, as also the digging of the grave; and I desire that W[illiam] T[uke] may take my clothes after my decease, and apply them accordingly.

John Woolman[2]

York, 29th of 9th month, 1772

In the Wisdom of Christ, O Joy!

Jesus has delivered himself entirely from himself, in order to be completely God's.[1]

Enfolded in the Love of God, we travel through our brokenness into a place of surrender and experience the cycles of crucifixion and resurrection, all the while approaching what is called death but what, in reality, is the transformation into eternal life.

As we hand more and more of ourselves over to God, our state of freedom grows deeper and we are more able to see God in all places; our joy deepens and we expect to see the goodness of God everywhere.

As John Woolman succumbed to the smallpox and approached his death, his recorded words are those of a soul in a state of almost complete freedom. But, like Christ on the cross, his human condition is clearly present.

This and the quotes that follow are John Woolman's words as recorded by William Tuke in his letter to Reuben Haines written on 26 October 1772.

> "Rejoice evermore, and in everything give thanks": but added a little after, "This is sometimes hard to come at."[2]

Nevertheless, John Woolman's connection with and abandonment to God is truly inspirational. Our Friend John Woolman, living and dying in the wisdom of Christ, desired to journey home to God.

"I looked round about, and was amazed in the depths of Misery. O Lord! I remembered that thou art Omnipotent; that I had called thee Father, and I felt that I loved thee; and I was made quiet in thy Will, and I waited for Deliverance from thee; Thou hadst pity upon me when no Man could help me; I saw that Meekness under Suffering, was showed unto us, in the most affecting example of thy Son, and thou wast teaching me to follow Him; and I said, thy will, O Father, be done." . . .

. . . "O my Father, my Father! How comfortable art thou to my Soul in this trying season!"

"I believe the Lord will now excuse me from Exercises of this kind, and I see now no Work but one, which is to be the last wrought by me in this World; the Messenger will come that will relieve me from all these troubles, but it must be in the Lord's Time, which I am waiting for. I have laboured to do whatever was required according to the Ability received, in the remembrance of which I have peace; and though the disorder is strong at Times and would come over my Mind like a Whirlwind yet it has hitherto been kept steady and centred in Everlasting Love, and if that is mercifully continued, I ask nor desire more."

"O Lord! it was thy Power that enabled me to forsake Sin in my Youth, and I have felt thy Bruises since for disobedience, but as I bowed under them, thou healest me; and though I have gone through many Trials and sore Afflictions, thou hast been with me, continuing a Father and a Friend. I feel thy Power now, and beg that in the approaching trying Moments, thou wilt keep my Heart stedfast unto thee."

"I had rather thou wouldest guard against Weeping and sorrowing for me, my Sister; I sorrow not, though I have had some painful Conflicts; but now they seem over, and Matters all settled; and I look at the Face of my

Dear Redeemer, for Sweet is his Voice and his countanance Comely."

"I believe my being here is in the Wisdom of Christ; I know not as to Life or Death."[3]

William Tuke wrote the following about John Woolman's final moments:

About a quarter before Six the same Morning, he seemed to fall into an easy sleep, which continued about half an Hour; when seeming to awake, he breathed a few Times with a little more difficulty, & so expired without Sigh, Groan or Struggle.[4]

Acknowledgements

This pilgrimage has been facilitated by the love of many people.

For the unconditional love of my grandmother, Granny Sorbie;
for my parents, Bill and Nan Lawson, who gave me everything they had;

for the decades of love from my intentional community of Isabel, Micah, Nick, Kaye, Graham, and my beloved wife Fi;

to Bill Taber who introduced me to John Woolman, and to all the staff at the libraries where I have carried out my research — the Historical Society of Pennsylvania, the Library Company (Philadelphia), the Quaker Collection at Swarthmore College, the Special Collection at Haverford College, and the Library at Friends House in London;

to Kenneth L. Carroll whose scholarship enabled me to spend a term at Pendle Hill in 1999 to explore the libraries mentioned above;

to Edward Sergeant and Pat Stewart in Philadelphia for their hospitality in their house of books, music and conversation

to Margaret Dwyer RSC, my spiritual director for over twenty years, now at home with God;

for the hospitality and conversations of Barbara and Sterling Olmsted;

to Doug Gwyn for the many conversations and encouragement during our travel to and from Haverford College and through the electronic ether in the years since;

and for the many unnamed people whose faithfulness has been life-sustaining for me;

from your brother on the winding path which is straighter than we think,

thank you.

Drew Lawson

NOTES

Meeting John Woolman (pp. iii–vii)

[1] Thomas Merton, *My Argument with the Gestapo: A Macaronic Journal* (New York: New Directions, 1975), 160–61.

John Woolman: Biographical Note (pp. 1–4)

[1] John Woolman, as quoted in Phillips P. Moulton, ed., *The Journal and Major Essays of John Woolman* (Richmond, IN: Friends United Press, 1989), 44.

[2] John Townsend to Sarah Woolman [1772], in Amelia Mott Gummere, ed., *The Journal and Essays of John Woolman* (New York: MacMillan Co., 1922), 149.

[3] *Leeds Mercury,* Oct. 13, 1772, in *Journal and Essays of John Woolman,* 144.

Sarah Woolman: Biographical Note (pp. 5–7)

[1] John Woolman to Sarah Woolman 31 July 1772, in Gummere, *Journal and Essays of John Woolman,* 133.

[2] Gummere, *Journal and Essays of John Woolman,* 39–40.

[3] Sarah Woolman to John Smith Jr., January 1776, in Gummere, *Journal and Essays of John Woolman,* 40–41.

Writing Letters (pp. 8–15)

[1] Ormerod Greenwood, "John Woolman and Susanna Lightfoot: His Unpublished Letter to Her," *Journal of the Friends Historical Society* 48, no. 4 (1957): 150.

[2] John Woolman to Sarah Woolman, 18 May 1760, in Gummere, *Journal and Essays of John Woolman,* 61.

[3] John Woolman to Sarah Woolman, 14 June 1760, in Gummere, *Journal and Essays of John Woolman,* 61.

[4] John Woolman to the Ely family, 9 May 1744. I read and transcribed the original handwritten letter in one of the four archives I visited while doing research for this book (see p. iii).

[5] Thomas Merton, *The Sign of Jonas* (London: Hollis & Carter, 1953), 129.

6 John Woolman to Susannah Lightfoot, after 1764, as quoted in Greenwood, "John Woolman and Susanna Lightfoot," 155–56.

7 William Tuke to Reuben Haines, 26 October 1772, in Gummere, *Journal and Essays of John Woolman*, 324.

John Woolman to the Ely Family, 9 May 1744 (pp. 16–18)

1 John Woolman to the Ely family, 9 May 1744. I read the original handwritten letter in one of the four archives I visited while doing research for this book (see p. iii).

The Rigorous Logic of Love (pp. 19–29)

1 John Woolman [1772], in Moulton, *Journal and Major Essays of John Woolman*, 184.

2 John Woolman to Sarah Woolman 24 April 1760, in Gummere, *Journal and Essays of John Woolman*, 232.

3 John Woolman to Sarah Woolman, 18 May 1760, in Gummere, *Journal and Essays of John Woolman*, 61.

4 Thomas Merton, *A Vow of Conversation: Journals, 1964–1965*, ed. Naomi Burton Stone (New York: Farrar Straus Giroux, 1988), 114.

5 John Woolman, probably to one of the Pemberton brothers or John Smith, late 1756, in Gummere, *Journal and Essays of John Woolman*, 185.

6 John Woolman, probably to one of the Pemberton brothers or John Smith, late 1756, in Gummere, *Journal and Essays of John Woolman*, 185–86.

7 Charles de Foucauld to Henri de Castries, as quoted in Madeleine Delbrêl, *The Joy of Believing*, trans. D. Ralph Wright (Sherbrooke, QC: Éditions Paulines, 1993), 28–29.

8 John Woolman to Elizabeth Smith, 28 April 1772, in William J. Allinson, comp., *Memorials of Rebecca Jones*, 2nd ed. (Philadelphia: Henry Longstreth, 1849), 30.

9 John Woolman, probably to one of the Pemberton brothers or John Smith, late 1756, in Gummere, *Journal and Essays of John Woolman*, 186.

10 John Woolman to Sarah Woolman, 24 April 1760, in Gummere, *Journal and Essays of John Woolman*, 232.

11 John Woolman to Sarah Woolman, 18 May 1760, in Gummere, *Journal and Essays of John Woolman*, 61.

¹² John Woolman to Sarah Woolman, 14 June 1760, in Gummere, *Journal and Essays of John Woolman*, 61–62.

¹³ John Woolman to Sarah Woolman, 23 June 1760, in Gummere, *Journal and Essays of John Woolman*, 68.

¹⁴ John Woolman to Sarah Woolman, 14 June 1760, in Gummere, *Journal and Essays of John Woolman*, 62.

¹⁵ John Woolman to Sarah Woolman, 23 June 1760, in Gummere, *Journal and Essays of John Woolman*, 68.

¹⁶ John Woolman to Rebecca Jones, 20 April 1762, Friends House Library, London.

¹⁷ John Woolman to Sarah Woolman, 8 June 1763, in Gummere, *Journal and Essays of John Woolman*, 88.

¹⁸ John Woolman to John and Mary Comfort, 28 April 1772, in Gummere, *Journal and Essays of John Woolman*, 122.

¹⁹ John Woolman to Rachel Wilson, 30 August 1772, in Gummere, *Journal and Essays of John Woolman*, 311.

²⁰ John Woolman, 20 June 1762. I read and transcribed the original handwritten letter in one of the four archives I visited while doing research for this book (see p. iii).

²¹ Merton, *A Vow of Conversation*, 113.

Letters: February 1755 to November 1763 (pp. 30–45)

¹ John Woolman to Catherine Payton, 25 February 1755. I read and transcribed the original handwritten letter in one of the four archives I visited while doing research for this book (see p. iii).

² John Woolman to John Smith, 21 June 1755. I read and transcribed the original handwritten letter in one of the four archives I visited while doing research for this book (see p. iii)

³ John Woolman, probably to one of the Pemberton brothers or John Smith, late 1756, in Gummere, *Journal and Essays of John Woolman*, 185–86.

⁴ John Woolman to Abraham Farrington, 1 October 1757, in *Friends Intelligencer* 14 (1858): 663. The paragraphs inside square brackets are in the original letter that I transcribed; they are not in the *Friends Intelligencer*'s edited version.

⁵ John Woolman to John Smith, 10 September 1758, in Gummere, *Journal and Essays of John Woolman*, 529.

⁶ John Woolman to John Smith, 16 April 1760, in Gummere, *Journal and Essays of John Woolman*, 59.

⁷ John Woolman to John Smith, 16 April 1760, in Gummere, *Journal and Essays of John Woolman*, 59.

[8] John Woolman to John Pemberton 16 April 1760, in Gummere, *Journal and Essays of John Woolman*, 60.

[9] John Woolman to Sarah Woolman, 24 April 1760, in Gummere, *Journal and Essays of John Woolman*, 232.

[10] John Woolman to John Smith, 11 May 1760, in Gummere, *Journal and Essays of John Woolman*, 60–61.

[11] John Woolman to Sarah Woolman, 18 May 1760, in Gummere, *Journal and Essays of John Woolman*, 61.

[12] John Woolman to Sarah Woolman, 14 June 1760, in Gummere, *Journal and Essays of John Woolman*, 61–62.

[13] John Woolman to John Smith, 17 June 1760, in Gummere, *Journal and Essays of John Woolman*, 63–64.

[14] John Woolman to Abner Woolman, 17 June 1760, in Gummere, *Journal and Essays of John Woolman*, 64.

[15] John Woolman to Sarah Woolman, 23 June 1760, in Gummere, *Journal and Essays of John Woolman*, 68.

[16] John Woolman to Jane Crosfield, 12 December 1760, in Gummere, *Journal and Essays of John Woolman*, 71.

Searching for John Woolman's Dead Kangaroo (pp. 46–57)

[1] John Woolman as quoted in William Tuke letter to Reuben Haines, 26 October 1772, in Gummere, *Journal and Essays of John Woolman*, 323–24.

[2] John Woolman to John Smith, 16 April 1760, in Gummere, *Journal and Essays of John Woolman*, 59.

[3] John Woolman to John Smith, 17 April 1760, in Gummere, *Journal and Essays of John Woolman*, 63.

[4] John Woolman to John Smith, 16 April 1760, in Gummere, *Journal and Essays of John Woolman*, 59.

[5] Reginald Reynolds, *The Wisdom of John Woolman*, as quoted in Moulton, *Journal and Major Essays of John Woolman*, 15.

[6] John Woolman to Israel Pemberton, 29 November 1763, as quoted in *Friends Journal*, Feb. 27, 1960, p. 136, https://archive.org/stream/friendthefriend06unse/friendthefriend06unse_djvu.txt.

[7] John Woolman, probably to one of the Pemberton brothers or John Smith, late 1756, in Gummere, *Journal and Essays of John Woolman*, 186.

[8] John Woolman to Sarah Woolman, 14 June 1760, in Gummere, *Journal and Essays of John Woolman*, 62.

⁹ John Woolman to Uriah Woolman, 4 June 1763. I read and transcribed the original handwritten letter in one of the four archives I visited while doing research for this book (see p. iii).

¹⁰ John Woolman to John Townsend, 19 June 1772, as quoted in Henry J. Cadbury, *John Woolman in England: A Documentary Supplement* (Philadelphia: Friends Historical Society, 1971), 53.

¹¹ Memorandum in John Woolman's account book written by Mary Woolman recording John Woolman's words, January 1770, in Gummere, *Journal and Essays of John Woolman*, 112.

¹² Memorandum in John Woolman's account book written by Aaron Smith about John Woolman, January 1770, in Gummere, *Journal and Essays of John Woolman*, 112.

¹³ John Woolman to Elizabeth Smith, 28 April 1772, in Gummere, *Journal and Essays of John Woolman*, 121. The paragraphs inside square brackets are in the original letter that I transcribed; they are not in Gummere's edited version.

¹⁴ John Woolman to John Wilson, 22 Sept 1772, in Gummere, *Journal and Essays of John Woolman*, 141.

¹⁵ John Woolman to John Wilson, 22 Sept 1772, in Gummere, *Journal and Essays of John Woolman*, 141.

¹⁶ Excerpt from journal [1720–1742], in Moulton, *Journal and Major Essays of John Woolman*, 25.

¹⁷ John Woolman to Susannah Lightfoot, after 1764, as quoted in Greenwood, "John Woolman and Susanna Lightfoot," 155.

¹⁸ John Woolman, probably to one of the Pemberton brothers or John Smith, late 1756, in Gummere, *Journal and Essays of John Woolman*, 185.

¹⁹ John Woolman to Susannah Lightfoot, after 1764, as quoted in Greenwood, "John Woolman and Susanna Lightfoot," 154.

²⁰ John Woolman to Israel Pemberton, 20 June 1762, in Gummere, *Journal and Essays of John Woolman*, 73.

²¹ Memorandum in John Woolman's account book written by Mary Woolman, quoting John Woolman, January 1770, in Gummere, *Journal and Essays of John Woolman*, 112.

Letters: 1761 to November 1763 (pp. 58–67)

¹ John Woolman to Hannah White 1761. I read and transcribed the original handwritten letter in one of the four archives I visited while doing research for this book (see p. iii).

² John Woolman to Israel Pemberton, 17 November 1761, in Gummere, *Journal and Essays of John Woolman*, 348.

3 John Woolman to Samuel Smith, 22 November 1761, in Gummere, *Journal and Essays of John Woolman*, 72.

4 John Woolman to Israel Pemberton, late 1761, , in Gummere, *Journal and Essays of John Woolman*, 349.

5 John Woolman to Israel Pemberton, 9 Febuary 1762, in Gummere, *Journal and Essays of John Woolman*, 349.

6 John Woolman to Rebecca Jones, 20 April 1762, Friends House Library, London.

7 John Woolman to Israel Pemberton, 20 June 1762, in Gummere, *Journal and Essays of John Woolman*, 73.

8 John Woolman to John Smith, 4 April 1763, in Gummere, *Journal and Essays of John Woolman*, 74.

9 John Woolman to Uriah Woolman, 4 June 1763. I read and transcribed the original handwritten letter in one of the four archives I visited while doing research for this book (see p. iii).

10 John Woolman to Sarah Woolman, 8 June 1763, in Gummere, *Journal and Essays of John Woolman*, 88.

11 John Woolman to Sarah Woolman and Israel Pemberton, 16 June 1763, in Gummere, *Journal and Essays of John Woolman*, 90.

12 John Woolman to Israel Pemberton, 27 June 1763, in Gummere, *Journal and Essays of John Woolman*, 91. The text inside square brackets is in the original letter that I transcribed; it is not in Gummere's edited version.

13 John Woolman to Israel Pemberton, 29 November 1763, in *Friends Journal*, Feb. 27, 1960, p. 136, https://archive.org/stream/friendthefriend06unse/friendthefriend06unse_djvu.txt.

14 John Woolman to Israel Pemberton, 30 November 1763. I read and transcribed the original handwritten letter in one of the four archives visite3d while doing research for this book (see p. iii).

Holy Obedience: Abandonment to God (pp. 68–79)

1 Merton, *A Vow of Conversation*, 117, emphasis in original.

2 John Woolman, "A Plea for the Poor," in Moulton, *Journal and Major Essays of John Woolman*, 241.

3 Excerpt from John Woolman's journal [1749–1756] in Moulton, *Journal and Major Essays of John Woolman*, 46.

4 Excerpt from John Woolman's journal [1757] in Moulton, *Journal and Major Essays of John Woolman*, 61.

5 Kathryn Damiano to author, 1998. Damiano was one of the founding facilitators for the School of the Spirit in North America.

6 John Woolman to Sarah Woolman, 24 April 1760, in Gummere, *Journal and Essays of John Woolman*, 232.

7 John Woolman, probably to one of the Pemberton brothers or John Smith, late 1756, in Gummere, *Journal and Essays of John Woolman*, 185.

8 Margaret O'Neal to author, ca. 1997.

9 Thomas Merton, *Thoughts in Solitude* (New York: Farrar Straus Giroux, 1999), 79.

10 John Woolman to Abraham Farrington, 1 October 1757, in *Friends Intelligencer* 14 (1858): 663.

11 John Woolman to Sarah Woolman, 13 June 1772, in Gummere, *Journal and Essays of John Woolman*, 130.

12 John Woolman to Israel Pemberton, 20 June 1762, in Gummere, *Journal and Essays of John Woolman*, 73.

13 John Woolman, probably to one of the Pemberton brothers or John Smith, late 1756, in Gummere, *Journal and Essays of John Woolman*, 186.

14 John Woolman to Israel Pemberton, 20 June 1762, in Gummere, *Journal and Essays of John Woolman*, 73.

15 John Woolman to John Smith, 11 May 1760, in Gummere, *Journal and Essays of John Woolman*, 60–61.

16 John Woolman to Sarah Woolman, 14 June 1760, in Gummere, *Journal and Essays of John Woolman*, in Gummere, *Journal and Essays of John Woolman*, 62.

17 John Woolman to Sarah Woolman, 23 June 1760, in Gummere, *Journal and Essays of John Woolman*, 68.

18 John Woolman to Sarah Woolman, 8 June 1763, in Gummere, *Journal and Essays of John Woolman*, 88.

19 John Woolman to Sarah Woolman, 16 June 1763, in Gummere, *Journal and Essays of John Woolman*, 90.

20 Thomas R. Kelly, *A Testament of Devotion* (New York: HarperCollins, 1992), 26.

21 John Woolman to "Beloved friend," ca. July 1768, in Gummere, *Journal and Essays of John Woolman*, 99.

22 John Woolman, probably to one of the Pemberton brothers or John Smith, late 1756, in Gummere, *Journal and Essays of John Woolman*, 185.

23 John Woolman to Sarah Woolman, 16 June 1763, in Gummere, *Journal and Essays of John Woolman*, 90.

24 John Woolman to unknown recipient, 9 July 1769, in Gummere, *Journal and Essays of John Woolman*, 99–100.

25 John Woolman, probably to one of the Pemberton brothers or John Smith, late 1756, in Gummere, *Journal and Essays of John Woolman*, 186.

26 St. Ignatius of Loyola, "Suscipe," Loyola Press, https://www.loyolapress.com/catholic-resources/prayer/traditional-catholic-prayers/saints-prayers/suscipe-prayer-saint-ignatius-of-loyola/.

Letters: April 1769 to January 1771 (pp. 80–87)

1 John Woolman to Israel Pemberton, 4 April 1769, Historical Society of Pennsylvania.

2 John Woolman to J. C., 10 May 1769. I read and transcribed the original handwritten letter in one of the four archives I visited while doing research for this book (see p. iii).

3 John Woolman to "Beloved friend," ca. July 1768, in Gummere, *Journal and Essays of John Woolman*, 98–99.

4 John Woolman to Israel Pemberton, 16 October 1769, in Cadbury, *John Woolman in England*, 34.

5 John Woolman to unknown recipient, 22 October 1769, Cadbury, *John Woolman in England*, 34.

6 John Woolman to John Pemberton, 11 November 1769, in Gummere, *Journal and Essays of John Woolman*, 110.

7 John Woolman to Israel Pemberton, 17 November 1769, in Gummere, *Journal and Essays of John Woolman*, 110.

8 Memorandum written by Mary Woolman recording the words of her father, John Woolman, 7 January 1770, in Gummere, *Journal and Essays of John Woolman*, 112.

9 Memorandum by John Woolman, 7 January 1770, in Gummere, *Journal and Essays of John Woolman*, 112.

10 Memorandum in John Woolman's account book recorded by Aaron Smith, January 1770, in Gummere, *Journal and Essays of John Woolman*, 112–13.

11 John Woolman with Israel Pemberton to Friends of the quarterly and monthly meetings, prior to 1771, in Gummere, *Journal and Essays of John Woolman*, 438, 440.

12 John Woolman to Israel Pemberton, 7 January 1771, in Gummere, *Journal and Essays of John Woolman*, 438.

13 John Woolman, testimony to Peter Harvey, 1771, in Gummere, *Journal and Essays of John Woolman*, 521–22.

Under a Sense of His Heavenly Love (pp. 88–97)

[1] John Woolman to Israel Pemberton, 20 June 1762, in Gummere, *Journal and Essays of John Woolman*, 73.

[2] John Woolman to John Smith, 11 May 1760, in Gummere, *Journal and Essays of John Woolman*, 61.

[3] John Woolman to John Wilson, 22 September 1772, in Gummere, *Journal and Essays of John Woolman*, 141.

[4] John Woolman to Elizabeth Smith, 28 April 1772, in Allinson, *Memorials of Rebecca Jones*, 30.

[5] Memorandum written by Mary Woolman recording the words of her father, John Woolman, 7 January 1770, in Gummere, *Journal and Essays of John Woolman*, 112.

[6] Memorandum in John Woolman's account book, second part written by Aaron Smith, January 1770, in Gummere, *Journal and Essays of John Woolman*, 112.

[7] John Woolman to John and Mary Comfort, 16 September 1772, in Gummere, *Journal and Essays of John Woolman*, 137.

[8] John Woolman to John and Mary Comfort, 16 September 1772, in Gummere, *Journal and Essays of John Woolman*, 137.

[9] John Woolman to John and Mary Comfort, 28 April 1772, in Gummere, *Journal and Essays of John Woolman*, 122.

[10] John Woolman to John Pemberton, 16 April 1760, in Gummere, *Journal and Essays of John Woolman*, 60.

[11] John Woolman to Israel Pemberton, 16 October 1769, in Cadbury, *John Woolman in England*, 34.

[12] John Woolman to Reuben and Margaret Haines, 31 July 1772, in Gummere, *Journal and Essays of John Woolman*, 134.

[13] John Woolman to Abner Woolman 17 June 1760, in Gummere, *Journal and Essays of John Woolman*, 64.

[14] John Woolman to Sarah Woolman, 23 June 1760, in Gummere, *Journal and Essays of John Woolman*, 68.

[15] John Woolman to Sarah Woolman 24 April 1760, in Gummere, *Journal and Essays of John Woolman*, 232.

[16] John Woolman to "Beloved friend," ca. July 1768, in Gummere, *Journal and Essays of John Woolman*, 98.

[17] John Woolman to Catherine Payton, 25 February 1755. I read and transcribed the original handwritten letter in one of the four archives I visited while doing research for this book (see p. iii).

[18] John Woolman to Jane Crosfield, 12 December 1760, in Gummere, *Journal and Essays of John Woolman*, 71.

[19] John Woolman to "Beloved friend," ca. July 1768, in Gummere, *Journal and Essays of John Woolman*, 98.

[20] John Woolman to "Beloved friend," ca. July 1768, in Gummere, *Journal and Essays of John Woolman*, 98.

[21] John Woolman to Uriah Woolman, 4 June 1763. I read and transcribed the original handwritten letter in one of the four archives I visited while doing research for this book (see p. iii).

[22] John Woolman to "Beloved friend," ca. July 1768, in Gummere, *Journal and Essays of John Woolman*, 98.

[23] John Woolman to Hannah White, 1761. I read and transcribed the original handwritten letter in one of the four archives I visited while doing research for this book (see p. iii).

[24] John Woolman to Israel Pemberton, late 1761, in Gummere, *Journal and Essays of John Woolman*, 349.

[25] John Woolman to Israel Pemberton, 9 Febuary 1762, in Gummere, *Journal and Essays of John Woolman*, 349.

[26] John Woolman to Friends of the quarterly and monthly meetings, 7 January 1771, in Gummere, *Journal and Essays of John Woolman*, 438, 440.

[27] John Woolman to J. C., 10 May 1769. I read and transcribed the original handwritten letter in one of the four archives I visited while doing research for this book (see p. iii).

[28] Excerpt from John Woolman's journal [1763] in Moulton, *Journal and Major Essays of John Woolman*, 130.

[29] John Woolman to Sarah Woolman, 8 June 1763, in Gummere, *Journal and Essays of John Woolman*, 88.

[30] Sarah Woolman to William Lightfoot, June 1763, in Gummere, *Journal and Essays of John Woolman*, 88–89.

[31] John Woolman to J. C., 10 May 1769. I read and transcribed the original handwritten letter in one of the four archives mentioned in the preface (see p. iii).

[32] John Woolman to Reuben & Margaret Haines, 23 September 1772, in Gummere, *Journal and Essays of John Woolman*, 141.

[33] John Woolman to Sarah Woolman, 14 June 1760, in Gummere, *Journal and Essays of John Woolman*, 62.

John Woolman to Susannah Lightfoot, Sometime after 1764 (pp. 98–105)

[1] John Woolman to Susannah Lightfoot, after 1764, as quoted in Greenwood, "John Woolman and Susanna Lightfoot," 150–56.

Crucifixion (pp. 106–114)

[1] John Woolman to Abraham Farrington, 1 October 1757, in *Friends Intelligencer* 14 (1858): 663.

[2] John Woolman to Abraham Farrington, 1 October 1757, in *Friends Intelligencer* 14 (1858): 663.

[3] John Woolman, probably to one of the Pemberton brothers or John Smith, late 1756, in Gummere, *Journal and Essays of John Woolman*, 185–86.

[4] Memorandum in John Woolman's account book, January 1770, in Gummere, *Journal and Essays of John Woolman*, 112.

[5] John Woolman to Hannah White, 1761. I read and transcribed the original handwritten letter in one of the four archives I visited while doing research for this book (see p. iii).

[6] John Woolman to Reuben and Margaret Haines, 14 June 1772, in Gummere, *Journal and Essays of John Woolman*, 131.

[7] John Woolman to Sarah Woolman, 31 July 1772, in Gummere, *Journal and Essays of John Woolman*, 133.

[8] John Woolman to John Smith, 16 April 1760, in Gummere, *Journal and Essays of John Woolman*, 59.

[9] John Woolman to Sarah Woolman, 13 June 1772, in Gummere, *Journal and Essays of John Woolman*, 130.

[10] John Woolman to Sarah Woolman, 24 April 1760, in Gummere, *Journal and Essays of John Woolman*, 232.

[11] John Woolman to John Smith, 16 April 1760, in Gummere, *Journal and Essays of John Woolman*, 59.

[12] John Woolman to Sarah Woolman, 14 June 1760, in Gummere, *Journal and Essays of John Woolman*, 61–62.

[13] John Woolman to Abner Woolman, 17 June 1760, in Gummere, *Journal and Essays of John Woolman*, 64.

[14] John Woolman to Israel Pemberton, 27 June 1772, in Gummere, *Journal and Essays of John Woolman*, 91.

[15] John Woolman to Sarah Woolman, 13 June 1772, in Gummere, *Journal and Essays of John Woolman*, 130.

[16] Page 116 letter to Sarah Woolman, 24 April 1760, in Gummere, *Journal and Essays of John Woolman*, 232.

[17] Page 117 letter to Jane Crosfield, 12 December 1760, in Gummere, *Journal and Essays of John Woolman*, 71.

[18] John Woolman to Uriah Woolman, 4 June 1763. I read and transcribed the original handwritten letter in one of the four archives I visited while doing research for this book (see p. iii).

[19] John Woolman to Sarah Woolman, 23 June 1760, in Gummere, *Journal and Essays of John Woolman*, 68.

[20] John Woolman to Jane Crosfield, 12 December 1760, in Gummere, *Journal and Essays of John Woolman*, 71.

[21] John Woolman, probably to one of the Pemberton brothers or John Smith, late 1756, in Gummere, *Journal and Essays of John Woolman*, 185.

[22] John Woolman to John Smith, 11 May 1760, in Gummere, *Journal and Essays of John Woolman*, 60–61.

[23] John Woolman to Sarah Woolman, 16 June 1763, in Gummere, *Journal and Essays of John Woolman*, 90.

Letters: April 1772 to September 1772 (pp. 115–124)

[1] John Woolman to Israel Pemberton, 15 April 1772, in Gummere, *Journal and Essays of John Woolman*, 119.

[2] John Woolman to Israel Pemberton Jr., April 1772, in Gummere, *Journal and Essays of John Woolman*, 119–20.

[3] John Woolman to John and Mary Comfort, 28 April 1772, in Allinson, *Memorials of Rebecca Jones*, 30–31.

[4] John Woolman to John and Mary Comfort, 28 April 1772, in Gummere, *Journal and Essays of John Woolman*, 122.

[5] John Woolman to Sarah Woolman, 13 June 1772, in Gummere, *Journal and Essays of John Woolman*, 130.

[6] John Woolman to Reuben and Margaret Haines, 14 June 1772, in Gummere, *Journal and Essays of John Woolman*, 131.

[7] John Woolman to John Woolman Jr., 14 June 1772, in Gummere, *Journal and Essays of John Woolman*, 131.

[8] John Woolman to John Townsend, 19 June 1772, "The Martha Spriggs Collection," *Journal of the Friends Historical Society* 29 (1932).

[9] John Woolman to John Townsend, 31 July 1772, in Gummere, *Journal and Essays of John Woolman*, 133.

[10] John Woolman to Sarah Woolman, 31 July 1772, in Gummere, *Journal and Essays of John Woolman*, 133.

[11] John Woolman to Reuben and Margaret Haines, 31 July 1772, in Gummere, *Journal and Essays of John Woolman*, 134.

[12] John Woolman to Rachel Wilson, 30 August 1772, in Gummere, *Journal and Essays of John Woolman*, 310–11.

[13] John Woolman to Rachel Wilson, 30 August 1772, "John Woolman to Rachel Wilson, 1772," *Journal of the Friends Historical Society* 22, no. 1 (1925), 18.

[14] John Woolman to John and Mary Comfort, 16 September 1772, in Gummere, *Journal and Essays of John Woolman*, 137.

[15] John Woolman to John Wilson, 22 September 1772, in Gummere, *Journal and Essays of John Woolman*, 141.

[16] John Woolman to Reuben and Margaret Haines, 23 September 1772, in Gummere, *Journal and Essays of John Woolman*, 141.

Deliverance from Bondage (pp.125–129)

[1] John Woolman to Susannah Lightfoot, after 1764, as quoted in Greenwood, "John Woolman and Susanna Lightfoot," 153.

[2] John Woolman to Susannah Lightfoot, after 1764, as quoted in Greenwood, "John Woolman and Susanna Lightfoot," 152.

[3] John Woolman to Susannah Lightfoot, after 1764, as quoted in Greenwood, "John Woolman and Susanna Lightfoot," 150–51.

[4] John Woolman, probably to one of the Pemberton brothers or John Smith, late 1756, in Gummere, *Journal and Essays of John Woolman*, 185–86.

[5] John Woolman to Susannah Lightfoot, after 1764, as quoted in Greenwood, "John Woolman and Susanna Lightfoot," 153.

[6] John Woolman, probably to one of the Pemberton brothers or John Smith, late 1756, in Gummere, *Journal and Essays of John Woolman*, 185.

[7] John Woolman to Susannah Lightfoot, after 1764, as quoted in Greenwood, "John Woolman and Susanna Lightfoot," 150.

[8] John Woolman to Susannah Lightfoot, after 1764, as quoted in Greenwood, "John Woolman and Susanna Lightfoot," 151.

[9] John Woolman to Susannah Lightfoot, after 1764, as quoted in Greenwood, "John Woolman and Susanna Lightfoot," 154–55.

William Tuke to Reuben Haines, 27 October 1772 (pp. 130–139)

[1] William Tuke to Reuben Haines, 26 October 1772, in Gummere, *Journal and Essays of John Woolman*, 317–25. The texts inside square brackets are from the original letter that I transcribed; they differ from or are not in Gummere's edited version.

[2] Memorandum dictated by John Woolman to William Tuke, 29 September 1772, in Gummere, *Journal and Essays of John Woolman*, 325.

In the Wisdom of Christ, O Joy! (pp. 140–142)

[1] Leonardo Boff, *Passion of Christ, Passion of the World: The Facts, Their Interpretation, and Their Meaning Yesterday and Today,* trans. Robert R. Barr (Maryknoll, NY: Orbis Books, 2011), 65.

[2] William Tuke to Reuben Haines, 26 October 1772, in Gummere, *Journal and Essays of John Woolman,* 322.

[3] Excerpts from letter from William Tuke to Reuben Haines, 26 October 1772, in Gummere, *Journal and Essays of John Woolman,* 319–24.

[4] William Tuke to Reuben Haines, 26 October 1772, in Gummere, *Journal and Essays of John Woolman,* 324.

Also available from Inner Light Books

A Call to Friends: Faithful Living in Desperate Times
By Marty Grundy
> ISBN 978–1-7346300–6-0 (hardcover)
> ISBN 978–1-7346300–7-7 (paperback)
> ISBN 978–1-7346300–8-4 (eBook)

Surrendering into Silence: Quaker Prayer Cycles
By David Johnson
> ISBN 978–1-7346300–0-8 (hardcover)
> ISBN 978–1-7346300–1-5 (paperback)
> ISBN 978–1-7346300–2-2 (eBook)

A Guide to Faithfulness Groups
By Marcelle Martin
> ISBN 978-1-7328239-4-5 (hardcover)
> ISBN 978-1-7328239-5-2 (paperback)
> ISBN 978-1-7328239-6-9 (eBook)

A Word from the Lost
By David Lewis
> ISBN 978-1-7328239-7-6 (hardcover)
> ISBN 978-1-7328239-8-3 (paperback)
> ISBN 978-1-7328239-9-0 (eBook)

William Penn's 'Holy Experiment'
by James Proud
> ISBN 978-0-9998332-9-2 (hardcover)
> ISBN 978-1-7328239-3-8 (paperback)

In the Stillness: Poems, prayers, reflections
by Elizabeth Mills
> ISBN 978-1-7328239-0-7 (hardcover)
> ISBN 978-1-7328239-1-4 (paperback)
> ISBN 978-1-7328239-2-1 (eBook)

Walk Humbly, Serve Boldly: Modern Quakers as Everyday Prophets
by Margery Post Abbott
> ISBN 978-0-9998332-6-1 (hardcover)
> ISBN 978-0-9998332-7-8 (paperback)
> ISBN 978-0-9998332-8-5 (eBook)

Primitive Quakerism Revived
by Paul Buckley
> ISBN 978-0-9998332-2-3 (hardcover)
> ISBN 978-0-9998332-3-0 (paperback)
> ISBN 978-0-9998332-5-4 (eBook)

Primitive Christianity Revived
by William Penn
Translated into Modern English by Paul Buckley

ISBN 978-0-9998332-0-9 (hardcover)
ISBN 978-0-9998332-1-6 (paperback)
ISBN 978-0-9998332-4-7 (eBook)

Jesus, Christ and Servant of God
Meditations on the Gospel According to John
by David Johnson

ISBN 978–0–9970604–6–1 (hardcover)
ISBN 978–0–9970604–7–8 (paperback)
ISBN 978–0–9970604–8–5 (eBook)

The Anti-War
by Douglas Gwyn

ISBN 978-0-9970604-3-0 (hardcover)
ISBN 978-0-9970604-4-7 (paperback)
ISBN 978-0-9970604-5-4 (eBook)

Our Life Is Love, the Quaker Spiritual Journey
by Marcelle Martin

ISBN 978-0-9970604-0-9 (hardcover)
ISBN 978-0-9970604-1-6 (paperback)
ISBN 978-0-9970604-2-3 (eBook)

A Quaker Prayer Life
by David Johnson

ISBN 978-0-9834980-5-6 (hardcover)
ISBN 978-0-9834980-6-3 (paperback)
ISBN 978-0-9834980-7-0 (eBook))

The Essential Elias Hicks
by Paul Buckley

ISBN 978-0-9834980-8-7 (hardcover)
ISBN 978-0-9834980-9-4 (paperback)
ISBN 978-0-9970604-9-2 (eBook)

The Journal of Elias Hicks
edited by Paul Buckley

ISBN 978-0-9797110-4-6 (hardcover)
ISBN 978-0-9797110-5-3 (paperback)

Dear Friend: The Letters and Essays of Elias Hicks
edited by Paul Buckley

ISBN 978-0-9834980-0-1 (hardcover)
ISBN 978-0-9834980-1-8 (paperback)

The Early Quakers and 'the Kingdom of God'
by Gerard Guiton

ISBN 978-0-9834980-2-5 (hardcover)
ISBN 978-0-9834980-3-2 (paperback)
ISBN 978-0-9834980-4-9 (eBook)

John Woolman and the Affairs of Truth
edited by James Proud

ISBN 978-0-9797110-6-0 (hardcover)
ISBN 978-0-9797110-7-7 (paperback)

Cousin Ann's Stories for Children by Ann Preston
edited by Richard Beards
illustrated by Stevie French

ISBN 978-0-9797110-8-4 (hardcover),
ISBN 978-0-9797110-9-1 (paperback)

Counsel to the Christian-Traveller: also Meditations and Experiences
by William Shewen

ISBN 978-0-9797110-0-8 (hardcover)
ISBN 978-0-9797110-1-5 (paperback)

CPSIA information can be obtained
at www.ICGtesting.com
Printed in the USA
BVHW032056111020
590795BV00006B/20/J